REFORMERS, TEACHERS, WRITERS

REFORMERS, TEACHERS, WRITERS

Curricular and Pedagogical Inquiries

NEAL LERNER

UTAH STATE UNIVERSITY PRESS
Logan

© 2019 by University Press of Colorado

Published by Utah State University Press
An imprint of University Press of Colorado
245 Century Circle, Suite 202
Louisville, Colorado 80027

 The University Press of Colorado is a proud member of
the Association of University Presses.

The University Press of Colorado is a cooperative publishing enterprise supported,
in part, by Adams State University, Colorado State University, Fort Lewis College,
Metropolitan State University of Denver, University of Colorado, University of Northern
Colorado, Utah State University, and Western Colorado University.

∞ This paper meets the requirements of the ANSI/NISO Z39.48-1992 (Permanence of
Paper).

ISBN: 978-1-60732-880-3 (paperback)
ISBN: 978-1-60732-881-0 (ebook)
DOI: https://doi.org/10.7330/9781607328810

Library of Congress Cataloging-in-Publication Data

Names: Lerner, Neal, author.
Title: Reformers, teachers, writers : curricular and pedagogical inquiries / Neal Lerner.
Description: Logan : Utah State University Press, [2018] | Includes bibliographical refer-
ences and index.
Identifiers: LCCN 2019005773 | ISBN 9781607328803 (pbk.) | ISBN 9781607328810
(ebook)
Subjects: LCSH: English language—Rhetoric—Study and teaching (Higher) | Composi-
tion (Language arts)—Study and teaching (Higher) | Universities and colleges—Cur-
ricula—United States. | High schools—Curricula—United States. | Education—United
States. | Writing centers—United States.
Classification: LCC PE1404 .L475 2018 | DDC 808/.0420711—dc23
LC record available at https://lccn.loc.gov/2019005773

Cover illustration © ESB Essentials / Shutterstock

CONTENTS

ACKNOWLEDGMENTS

The varied inquiries in this book represent over ten years of reading, writing, researching, thinking, talking, bike riding, running, and writing some more. Many friends, colleagues, and family members have played significant roles. Michael Spooner at Utah State University Press was a vital early supporter and enabler of this project. Rachael Levay at USUP smoothly picked up the trail from Michael and was a pleasure to work with. Two anonymous reviewers provided essential feedback to an earlier version of this book. Anne Ellen Geller and Michele Eodice, my friends and coauthors, challenge me to avoid safe conclusions and provide needed strong drink and conversation. My Northeastern University colleagues Mya Poe, Chris Gallagher, Beth Britt, and Ellen Cushman are all models of professional grace, curiosity, and wit. Kyle Oddis was essential to the research in chapter 7 and a future leader in writing center studies. Michael Dedek got me thinking about the nature of curriculum in writing studies, and Michael Turner and Heather Falconer offered me opportunities to reflect on my own professional growth and the mentoring of PhD students. Many thanks, too, to Sarah Platanitis, a fine and inspiring teacher. Also thanks to Anne Herrington, Christiane Donahue, Chuck Bazerman, Chris Anson, Cinthia Gannett, John Brereton, Tom Deans, Ann Dean, Steve Slaner, Sandra Clyne, and Xinghua Li, all of whom offered feedback and support at various stages of this project. Kudos to the staffs at Peets Coffee and Caffé Nero in Brookline and to the Brookline Public Library (Coolidge Corner and Brookline Village locations) for providing terrific writing environments. Finally, the love and support of Tania Baker, Hannah Baker-Lerner, and Clay Baker-Lerner make this work worthwhile.

Earlier versions of portions of this book were previously published in *Writing on the Edge* ("Cultivating Habits for Success," copyright 2017 by the University of California Davis, reprinted with permission) and *Pedagogy: Critical Approaches to Teaching Literature, Language, Composition, and Culture* ("Resilience and Resistance in Writing Center Theory and Practice," copyright 2018 by Duke University, reprinted with permission). Archival material appears courtesy of the University of California Berkeley Music Library. Partial funding came from a Massachusetts Institute of Technology, Dean of Humanities Arts and Social Sciences Research Grant.

REFORMERS, TEACHERS, WRITERS

INTRODUCTION

Like many who teach college writing for a living, I started my career as an adjunct faculty member, first in California, then in Maryland for a few years, then in Massachusetts. In my first year, 1989, I was a California "freeway flyer," driving my old Volkswagon Squareback between Menlo Park and San Jose, from first-year writing at several community colleges to basic writing at San Jose State. When my car died one day on the Junipero Serra Highway, a piston seizing in an engine that leaked oil like the proverbial sieve, I then took the commuter rail and strategically parked a bicycle at each train station, scurrying to class with a messenger bag full of books and student papers.

I upgraded my commuting arrangement once I moved to Maryland, where I drove my wife's Toyota Tercel some 400 miles a week to teaching gigs at several community colleges and at the University of Maryland University College (UMUC), an arm of the University of Maryland system that catered to working adults and members of the military, with, at the time, 95,000 students worldwide. UMUC was a pioneer in distance education, and the great bulk of this teaching was done by adjunct faculty.

Once we moved to Massachusetts in fall 1992, I was a full-time student in a doctoral of education program and continued my life as an adjunct, pushing that Toyota Tercel through the last two years of its life to teaching gigs at colleges in and outside of route 128 and through the city to UMass Boston. That teaching ranged from creative writing for learning-disabled adults to research writing in a competency-based degree program to first-year composition and literature in an all-women's (at the time) college.

This variety of courses marked my life as an adjunct, as it does for most adjunct instructors, willing to take on what we are given. Typically during this period, I was handed a curriculum complete with readings, writing assignments, due dates and, in some cases, prerecorded lectures on audiocassettes (it was quite a while ago). I liked teaching these classes, perhaps because I liked the curriculum and felt that I was learning the material alongside my students, whether the subject was Victorian literature or business communication or twentieth-century

DOI: 10.7330/9781607328810.c000

film (and, of course, such "teacher-proof" materials ensured that a wide swath of adjuncts would be able to teach these classes). I could also be creative about how to structure students' learning experiences around and within this curriculum, whether that was how I used class time or, for classes that were essentially independent learning with few structured whole-class meetings, how I responded to students' drafts in order to encourage revision and a reengagement with that curriculum. In other words, I was in control of how I taught, in control of pedagogy, putting into practice what I believed were the best ways for students to interact with and learn from that curriculum. I was a writing teacher whose training in writing process pedagogies allowed me to do what I felt best equipped to do: ensure that students engaged in invention, drafting, and revision; structure discussions, debates, and interactions with the course material; respond to students' writing as a reader genuinely interested in students' ideas and how they might better express those ideas in subsequent drafts or in the next writing assignment. At this point, just a few years and a handful of classes into my teaching career, it was a relief to be able to focus just on these pedagogical elements. The curriculum was chugging along just fine without me.

Nearly thirty years later, I'm not so sure.

On the most basic level, the difference between curriculum and pedagogy is the difference between what is taught and how it is taught: between content and instruction. However, curriculum is not merely assigned texts and topics for reading and writing, and pedagogy isn't just about classroom or tutoring strategies. Instead, curriculum is dynamic and socially constituted, the process and product of the interaction between teachers, students, and materials, and the result of strategic choices in and outside of the classroom. Curriculum is influenced by textbook publishers, state legislators, schoolteachers and principals, college faculty and their committees. Curriculum is how education in the United States can be an assertion and replication of the status quo while also presenting a challenge to status quo values and hierarchies. It is both authoritarian and transgressive, constraining and enabling, hidden and transparent. The dynamic between pedagogy and curriculum is how a teacher scaffolds students' learning experiences, and how students bring to bear their previous knowledge and goals for their own learning to create new knowledge. In short, pedagogy and curriculum are interrelated, and progress is not possible if we are attentive only to one and not the other.

Most important, however, is that curriculum and pedagogy do not have equal weight—the scales are decidedly tipped in favor of curriculum. At my university, we have "curriculum committees" at department, college, and university levels; we do not have "pedagogy committees." Curriculum is what college faculty "own," develop, debate, vote on, and approve. It's what accrediting agencies scrutinize. It's a large part of what disciplines are defined by—the constructed knowledge that reaches back to those who came before and forward to new dimensions of knowledge making not yet imagined. Teaching practices—pedagogies—are certainly important to the enterprise of disciplinarity, but on their own they have little authority. This doesn't refer merely to the old saw of the brilliant scientist who is an awful teacher; it speaks to the ways teaching is largely devalued by a system of higher (and K–12) education that strives to pay as little as possible for teaching expertise and is dependent on an economic model in which the majority of teaching—particularly the teaching of writing—is performed by adjunct, part-time instructors, ones who rarely have any role in the development of curriculum.

Let me back up. The problem is not necessarily that we in the field of writing studies leave curriculum largely unchallenged or in the hands of textbook publishers, school boards, and state legislators (though we largely do). The problem is that we do not distinguish between curriculum and pedagogy or, more critically, that we are reluctant to address curriculum. In classrooms from kindergarten to college, writing teachers have largely come to a common understanding of pedagogy in their teaching. More specifically, a belief in "writing as a process" or the "process movement" or the very sensible notion that most writing requires periods of idea generation, writing, and revising—all dependent on meaningful feedback—has taken hold over the last thirty-five years. Of course, such sensibilities clash with onetime high-stakes writing exams, standardized assessments, and labor conditions in which a single high school or two-year college teacher is faced with responding to the drafts of her 125 students. While the conditions for ideal process-oriented classrooms and school systems remain elusive, I would bet that a glimpse into a classroom in which writing is the primary endeavor would look pretty similar from the late 1970s to now. In other words, in writing classrooms, we have carefully developed and can largely agree on "writing process pedagogies," or the activities we ask students to engage in and the practices of learning and teaching writing, but *what* students might be reading and writing about and the relationship between those topics for writing and our teaching practices are far less defined. Our inattention to curriculum ultimately hampers our effort to enact meaningful reform and to have an impact on larger conversations about education and writing. In short, the barrier to reform that I focus on in this book is our field's conflation of curriculum and pedagogy when we should be treating the two as separate and important (though thoroughly intertwined) components.

The current educational climate seems ripe for reform efforts, the latest version of Johnny can't write, think, compute, or calculate. Writing (or the lack thereof) comes into particularly strong focus in Arum and Roksa's *Academically Adrift* (2010), in which we're told that most students do not write or read much in their first three semesters of college and consequently do not show improved performance by the end of their sophomore years—at least on the Collegiate Learning Assessment. This push-pull of educational reform—efforts to improve responding to evidence of failure—is seemingly hardwired into the system. Back in 1985, Mike Rose ascribed the cause of these recurring cycles to "the myth of transience," or the belief of English teachers and policy makers that "the past was better or that the future will be. The turmoil they are currently in will pass" (356). This belief, in Rose's words, "blinds faculty members to historical reality and to the dynamic and fluid nature of the educational system that employs them" (356). Other writers have taken up Rose's "myth of transience" to explain the lack of progress in writing reform, perhaps most notably David Russell (1991) in his history of writing across the curriculum (27). The belief in the myth of transience—for teachers, would-be reformers, and critics—contributes to a situation in which the next "crisis" in students' literacy skills always seems imminent, in which professional organizations and national commissions repeatedly call for change, but in which real change rarely takes hold.

While no doubt powerful, the belief that the present moment is not connected to the past or future does not seem enough to explain the ways that student writing performance seems always in crisis, imperiled by lax standards, informality, and the allure of technology (whether radio in the 1930s, television in the 1960s, or Reddit and Snapchat in our present age). Understanding the persistence of *the problem* of student writing—and thus *the problem* of writing instruction—requires more than belief in a myth—instead we must understand the very real barriers to institutional and instructional reform, whether those barriers are political, institutional, pedagogical, curricular, or personal.

Perhaps this reluctance to engage in curricular reform is the legacy of previous largely unsuccessful curricular efforts, such as the post-Sputnik, federally funded Project English in the 1960s (Lerner 2009, ch. 5) or the recent P-16 movement to align curriculum from preschool to college (Davis and Hoffman 2008) or the long-standing belief that curriculum is largely a local issue—or at least within the bounds of state standards and curriculum guides. Or perhaps our reluctance is an effect of the 1980s and 1990s culture wars over curriculum in the college writing classroom, whether radiating out from Linda Brodkey's experiences at University of Texas, Austin (1994) and the associated writing studies debate over the role of "politics" in the composition classroom (e.g., Hairston 1992), legacies of 1980s "great books" bromides from E. D. Hirsch (1987) and William Bennett (1996), or the successful movement to fill local school boards with conservative standard-bearers. Whatever the causes, our expertise with pedagogy and "writing as a process" emerges as the staple of the field, and that conclusion is considered perfectly tolerable in a climate that allows "writing as a process" to somehow define an entire discipline. But such definitions are only partial, only the shell of a discipline without substantial disciplinary content and certainly without any means to enact meaningful institutional reform.

To look for evidence of our field's attention to pedagogy versus curriculum, I ran a Google Ngram search (https://books.google.com/ngrams) for the occurrence of the phrases "writing process" versus "writing curriculum" from 1900 to 2000. As shown in figure 0.1, neither term appears with much frequency in the Google books database until around 1950, when "writing process" begins to take off and then dramatically increases from around 1970 until the late 1990s, when it levels off; "writing curriculum," however, never receives more than a few mentions.

In literature intended to represent the collected knowledge of the field, writing curriculum similarly receives short shrift in comparison to writing pedagogy. For example, the second edition of *The Guide to Composition Pedagogies* (Tate et al. 2013) was released in 2013 (the first edition came out in 2000); however, a companion *Guide to Composition Curriculum* does not exist. Further, the edited collection *Keywords in Composition Studies* (Heilker and Vandenberg), published in 1996, includes "pedagogy" as one of those keywords, but not "curriculum." In that volume, attention to the processes of writing comes with the words "composing/writing," "process," and "revision," but one is hard-pressed to discover what it is that students might be composing/writing/processing/revising. More recent articulation of writing studies as a discipline as represented in the collection *Composition, Rhetoric, & Disciplinarity* (Malenczyk et al. 2018) similarly gives short shrift to curriculum: the term does not appear at all in the index, while "pedagogy" garners five references. Indeed, in their introduction to the book, the editors note that "we are today a pedagogically focused field" (7). A concomitant declaration of the curriculum of the field, an essential component of what might constitute a discipline, does not appear.

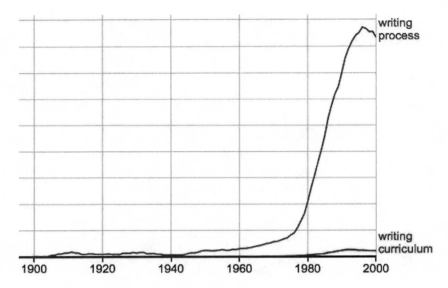

Figure 0.1. Google Ngram comparison of frequency of occurrence of "writing process" versus "writing curriculum," 1900–2000

Perhaps articulation of curriculum might be found in another recent collection, *Naming What We Know: Threshold Concepts of Writing Studies* (Adler-Kassner and Wardle 2015), which draws from Meyer and Land's (2003) notion that a "threshold concept" is "a transformed way of understanding, or interpreting, or viewing something without which the learner cannot progress" (1).[1] The "something" referred to in this collection might offer evidence as to what curriculum might look like in writing studies, particularly a curriculum essential for entry to and progress in the field. Indeed, convincing readers to teach the threshold concepts is the primary project of this book (and perhaps even more so in the subsequent "classroom edition" [Adler-Kassner and Wardle 2016]). This codified body of knowledge represents a strong disciplinary claim: writing studies, like any discipline, is built on "threshold concepts," and such conceptual knowledge should be the core of continued study in the field, just as it is in more visible and established fields.

Still, what troubles me about this approach to creating curriculum is the absence of students' input and the regulatory inevitability of codified concepts (despite Yancey's claims in the book's introduction that threshold concepts do not represent a "canon" but instead are "contingent" [Yancey 2015, xix]) as well as a lack of attention to the relationship between pedagogy and curriculum. One might teach threshold concepts in first-year writing, for example, as Downs and Robertson (2015) describe in this collection, making "threshold concepts the declarative content of the course" (105). The intended curricular outcome is a "framework to which students can transfer revised or reimagined prior knowledge, from which they can transfer new or reconceptualized knowledge to a wide range of writing situations, and with which they can understand that the nature of learning (especially that which they'll see throughout college) is inquiry based and troublesome yet potentially transformative, thus opening themselves to greater potential for that learning to occur" (119).

The knowledge being referenced here is knowledge about how writing "works" or has worked in students' prior, present, and future experiences. Not described, however, is what exactly students might be writing about other than analysis at the metaconceptual level (as well as a lack of concrete evidence that such an approach might be more effective than any other). There's a decidedly evangelical angle here: the explicit goal of having students become true believers in the applicability of the threshold concept framework to any subject or to future classes in which writing will play a strong role. The message is that it is not merely students' knowledge about writing that might be "revised," "reconceptualized," or "transferred"—their very identities as learners might be similarly transformed. These ambitious goals, however, largely take a deficit stance toward students (i.e., they need to be "revised" and "reconceptualized") and largely ignore the many resources students bring to their writing, namely, the passions, interests, histories, and aspirations that offer "personal connections" and that might make their writing meaningful (Eodice, Geller, and Lerner 2016). A truly collaborative and consequential approach to curriculum in first-year writing—or any class in which writing plays a significant role—needs to make central what students bring to their learning and the ways that these "incomes" (Guerra 2008) are strongly connected to meaningful writing experiences.

I also believe that attention to curriculum in writing studies is essential for delivering on writing studies' intentions to make our classrooms, writing centers, and community spaces inclusive of diverse learners. While the Conference on College Composition and Communication's (CCCC) endorsement of students' "right to their own languages" dates to 1974, the essential role of students in determining the curriculum (or the "right to their own curriculum") of their college writing courses is far less articulated or acknowledged. While students might have some degree of choice when it comes to topics for writing (though navigating "banned topics" lists is commonplace, particularly in first-year writing), they are typically writing in highly constrained environments, ones in which they had little to no say in what those constraints might look like. The curricular partnership with students that I am calling for in this book starts with the negotiation between our goals as teachers and students' goals as learners, between our histories as writers and teachers of writing and students' histories as writers and as family and community members, and their hopes and dreams for what their educations might produce. While K–12 educators have spent decades developing "culturally relevant curricula" (Aronson and Laughter, 2016), in post-secondary education, particularly in required writing classes, what often prevails is curriculum driven by the mastery of particular forms of writing, with occasional spaces for students to insert their interests and passions—as long as the fit conforms to the given spaces.[2]

As I describe throughout this book, articulation of curriculum—or at least a process by which we transparently create curriculum alongside our students—is essential to fulfill writing studies' disciplinary aspirations. Perhaps more important, however, is that curriculum is an assertion of values. Such assertions can easily be found in our professional statements, in our commitments to social justice, diversity, and inclusion, and in our research that shows the powerful roles that writing plays to shape/limit/make possible individual and communal agency. We work at odds with our good intentions when our design of curriculum and the curriculum itself do not reflect these values. The result is an uncomfortable relationship between who we are as a field and who we want to be, a gap that can account for the continued failure of our reform efforts.

In *Reformers, Teachers, Writers: Curricular and Pedagogical Inquiries*, I explore the distinction between curriculum and pedagogy in writing studies—and how failing to attend to that distinction largely results in the failure of educational reform. My sites of inquiry for these explorations are many and varied: current professional statements about college readiness and assertions of curriculum for "writing about writing"; stories from the first third of my teaching career when I was a student teacher in two San Jose–area high schools and then an adjunct writing instructor in community colleges and universities, teaching students ranging from basic writers in community colleges to nuclear power plant employees to Ford automotive technicians; descriptions of two students from my history as a teacher, both of whom embraced the "extracurriculum" —or took curricular matters into their own hands, so to speak —and are both now serving federal prison sentences for terrorist activities; the late-nineteenth-century Holyoke, Massachusetts, public schools, where a newly hired superintendent would stress instructional reform, namely, individualized and "laboratory" approaches to instruction, only to be run out of office by an entrenched status quo uneasy with reform; contemporary Holyoke High School, where a majority minority student population and their junior-year English literature teacher struggle to fulfill the curriculum requirements of a literary analysis project; contemporary writing centers or sites best known for their pedagogical approaches to teaching writing but where a largely invisible curriculum shapes every interaction. I conclude with what I hope to see as the future of writing studies and educational reform.

This mixed-methods approach—using quantitative, qualitative, textual, historical, narrative, and theoretical methods—reflects the importance and effects of curriculum in a wide variety of settings, whether writing centers, writing classrooms, or students' out-of-school lives, as well as the many methodological approaches available to understand curriculum in writing studies. I believe that the richness of this approach allows for multiple considerations of the distinction (and relationship) between pedagogy and curriculum. Thus, what might seem at first to be disparate considerations are instead brought together by the central focus on curriculum and its importance in the many contexts in which writing plays a role. Further, I group chapters into three parts: (1) disciplinary inquiries, (2) experiential inquiries, and (3) empirical inquiries, exploring the presence and effect of curriculum and its relationship to pedagogy in multiple sites, both historical and contemporary, and for multiple stakeholders.

PART 1: DISCIPLINARY INQUIRIES

CHAPTER 1: WHAT IS CURRICULUM, ANYWAY? Drawing on educational theory, in this chapter I offer a robust definition of curriculum, including what an instructor might intend based on an example syllabus, as well as what she does not intend but what students might experience. An important distinction is between the curriculum that is "delivered" and curriculum that is "developed," with the latter offering opportunity for student agency and consideration of student "incomes."

CHAPTER 2: READY OR NOT, HERE WE CURRICULUM. As examples of the lack of definition of curriculum in the teaching of writing and its consequences, in this chapter, I turn to three recent efforts: (1) *The Framework for Success in Postsecondary Writing* (Council of Writing Program Administrators, National Council of Teachers of English, and the National Writing Project 2011), our professional organizations' attempts to assert expertise in national conversations on the topic of "college readiness"; (2) the Council of Writing Program Administrators' "Outcomes Statement for First-Year Composition" (2014); and (3) the effort to create content and curriculum for first-year writing via the "writing about writing" (WAW) approach (Wardle and Downs 2014). My critique of each of these examples primarily centers on the long-standing tendency to blame students for their lack of learning, their lack of readiness, their lack of engagement, or their lack of knowledge transfer. The overwhelming message is that responsibility is an individual one—these efforts place responsibility for success clearly with the individual student, not the social context, not the classroom, not the institution, and just barely with the teacher.

PART 2: EXPERIENTIAL INQUIRIES

CHAPTER 3: LEARNING TO TEACH AS A FREEWAY FLYER. My career as a writing teacher began with two semesters of student teaching for my high school English credential and then eight years of adjunct assignments in higher education. From northern California to the Washington, DC, area to Boston, I taught as many as seven classes a semester and worked with students from Ford automotive technicians to nuclear power plant operators to community college returning adults to university freshmen. The ways that these experiences emphasized pedagogy, often at the expense of curriculum, particularly when curriculum was largely out of my hands as a "freeway flyer" quickly moving from one teaching gig to the next, offer a challenge to our field, given its strong reliance on part-time adjunct teachers.

CHAPTER 4: TEACHING AND TUTORING TERRORISTS. Biswanath Halder was convicted in 2005 of terrorist activities, including manslaughter, when he stormed a building on the campus of Case Western Reserve University and shot an innocent bystander. Tarek Mehanna was convicted in 2012 of "conspiracy to provide material support to terrorists." Both men are serving federal prison sentences. Biswanath Halder was a writing center client of mine when I worked as a writing consultant at Boston University. Tarek Mehanna was a student of mine at the Massachusetts College of Pharmacy & Health Sciences in Boston. Both of my former students took curriculum into their own hands, albeit in different ways, both using writing as a means of seeking justice and action. This chapter considers the role of the extracurriculum, or the writing curriculum outside of our classrooms, and the ways that the consequences of our teaching can never quite be known.

PART 3: EMPIRICAL INQUIRIES

CHAPTER 5: PRESTON SEARCH AND THE POLITICS OF EDUCATIONAL REFORM. This archival inquiry into the relationship between pedagogy and curriculum is set in Holyoke, Massachusetts. As the superintendent of schools in Holyoke in the mid-1890s, Preston Search brought radical ideas of teaching reform. Specifically, he advocated nonauthoritarian, student-centered classrooms, ones built around students' individual needs, rather than mass instruction in what the system deemed most worth knowing. In the largely immigrant urban Holyoke, his ideas met resistance from the entrenched political elite, and his stay as superintendent was relatively brief. One lesson from Search's story is that pedagogical reform has as many limits as curricular reform, particularly given the politics of urban schooling and the strength of the status quo.

CHAPTER 6: LEARNING TO WRITE AT HOLYOKE HIGH. This chapter presents a qualitative study of one semester in the life of a Holyoke High School English teacher. As was true in Search's time, contemporary Holyoke is a city of immigrants, and Ms. T, in her second year in the school, finds that her largely student-centered and creative pedagogy conflicts in large and small ways with the traditional curricular requirements and students' own reluctance to make the curricular materials their own.

CHAPTER 7: THE HIDDEN CURRICULUM OF WRITING CENTERS. This chapter offers a quantitative and textual analysis of curriculum in what might be an unlikely place: the university writing center. In what is seen as largely a pedagogical space (Boquet 1999), the presence of curriculum is nevertheless strong, particularly in the co-construction (and potential clash) of knowledge that is at the heart of the writing tutorial. More specifically, I analyze online, synchronous writing center sessions for the presence of knowledge claims by tutor and student and the ways those claims range from monologic to dialogic and assert knowledge about tutor and student roles, about the writing process, and about the role of emotion in writing and tutoring. Bringing visibility to writing center curriculum offers the opportunity for writing centers to "name what we know" and assert a disciplinary presence.

CHAPTER 8: THE FUTURE OF CURRICULUM IN WRITING STUDIES. In this book, I have shown that a significant barrier to change is our lack of attention to curriculum or the conflation of pedagogy with curriculum. In this final chapter, I outline possible directions for needed attention to curriculum, representing a commitment to co-construct curriculum with students, colleagues, and institutions.

NOTES

1. In the interest of full disclosure, I need to note that I am a contributor to *The Guide to Composition Pedagogies*, 2nd ed, to *Naming What We Know*, both the full edition and the classroom edition, and to *Composition, Rhetoric, & Disciplinarity*.

2. A counter to this classroom environment filled with constraints are the long-standing calls for language difference, particularly the relationship between students' home languages and the languages of schooling, to be central to what happens in a writing classroom (though it is quite rare for these authors to describe their recommended approaches as "curricular"). See, for instance, Alexander and Rhodes 2012; Canagarajah 2006; Horner et al. 2011; Kinloch 2005; Lu 1998; Smitherman 2003; and Villanueva 1993.

PART 1

Disciplinary Inquiries

1
WHAT IS CURRICULUM, ANYWAY?

As I described in the introduction, my career as a college writing teacher started in California, then shifted to Maryland when my wife took a position as a postdoctoral fellow at the National Institutes of Health in Bethesda. I arrived in Bethesda in July 1990, and by that fall semester, I was hired to teach developmental and first-year writing (three sections total) at Frederick Community College as well as a section of Critical Thinking and Writing and a section of Exploring Language: Thinking, Writing, Communicating at the University of Maryland University College (UMUC), which largely served returning adults and active military. This volume of teaching and of preparation for different kinds of writing courses would continue for the two-plus years I lived in Maryland:

- Spring 1991: four sections total at two different community colleges and UMUC.
- Fall 1991: four sections total at Frederick Community College and UMUC.
- Spring 1992: seven sections total (and six different preparations!) at two different community colleges and UMUC.
- Summer 1992: two sections total at UMUC.

Now, while most of the sections at UMUC did not require multiple weekly class meetings (UMUC was a pioneer in various forms of distance education), I was still commuting over 400 miles per week with my wife's Toyota Tercel, struggling with DC Beltway traffic, and managing the workload of responding to the writing of 100 students or more per semester. While I did not have much choice at the time—postdoc salaries and per-course adjunct pay are notoriously low, and our rent in Bethesda was high—it was clear that this volume of teaching was not sustainable. I began to apply for full-time community college positions, but before I could fully immerse myself in that process, I realized that my future prospects could be greatly enhanced if I were to pursue additional graduate study (a somewhat painful decision considering that I was still paying off my undergraduate

DOI: 10.7330/9781607328810.c001

student loans as well as the loans I incurred for my MA and secondary English credential degrees). The timing was also key: my wife had accepted a faculty position in the Boston area starting in fall 1992, so we would be moving to Boston, and I began to look into doctoral programs there.

At the time, I knew very little about graduate study in rhetoric and composition, despite how much I had liked these courses in my MA program. I figured that an English PhD would mean the study of literature, in which I had little interest. Further, my community college teaching experiences in California and Maryland had exposed me to the diverse learners and social missions of those institutions, and the two summers I spent as a teaching fellow at two different National Writing Project sites (San Jose and Northern Virginia) had expanded my repertoire as a writing teacher and given me meaningful exposure to teacher research. These experiences, combined with the liberatory pedagogy emphasis of my secondary education credential program, pointed to a doctoral program in education as the best path forward. So that's what I did.

My first dip into those waters occurred at the College of Notre Dame (CND) in Baltimore, where I enrolled in a certificate program in curriculum and instruction while we still lived in Maryland. I figured this experience would help bolster my applications to education doctoral programs in the Boston area, given that my degrees at that point were in English and that my high school teaching experience had not advanced beyond student teaching. The CND faculty were religious and lay professionals dedicated to education as a means of enacting social justice, and my classmates were a dynamic group of inner-city teachers seeking professional development opportunities. What I learned over two semesters at CND was that "curriculum" and "instruction" were two separate but related concepts. By the time I enrolled in Boston University's education doctorate program in 1992, I was in a cohort of classmates, many of whom were, once again, in the curriculum and instruction strand (I was in "Development Studies: Literacy, Language, & Cultural Studies," which seemed most suitable to me when it came time to choose). Starting with my first semester, I was a teaching assistant in a Foundations of Education survey class, and treatment of "curriculum" as distinct from "instruction" was the status quo.

My travels through the educational landscape over the next twenty-five-plus years took me farther and farther away from schools and departments of education. Nevertheless, the distinction and relationship between curriculum and instruction in writing studies have been gnawing at me—or, more accurately, I have long been concerned with the lack of an explicit articulation of curriculum. In this chapter, I offer that articulation by drawing on educational theory and apply that definition of curriculum to my syllabus from a recent first-year writing class.

WHAT CURRICULUM IS AND IS NOT

Curriculum can be narrowly conceived as "subjects of study" or content in any course. That content—often expressed in a syllabus as specific reading and writing tasks or unit topics—is an important component of curriculum. However, in this book I draw on a much more expansive definition, largely from the K–12 educational literature. For one expansive definition of curriculum, I turn to Nieto et al. (2008), who write that "we view curriculum as including not only texts, but also other instructional materials, programs, projects, physical environments for learning, interactions among teachers and students, and all the intended and unintended messages about expectations, hopes, and dreams that students, their communities, and schools have about student learning and the very purpose of schools" (176). In other words, curriculum consists of the complex relationship between subjects of study, learning environments, and learners' and teachers' histories, motivations, and aspirations, among other factors. Ayers et al. (2008) introduce in their definition the ways that curriculum is also political and inextricably tied to issues of power and authority:

> Is the curriculum a mandate or is it learning as it is engaged on the ground? Is the curriculum immutable, or is it a dynamic and living thing? Is it a course of study, a body of knowledge, a scope and sequence, a set of settled objectives or directives from those who know best? Is the curriculum a political or a pedagogical thing? Teachers' encounter with and experience of curriculum encompass all of these shadings and more—and those who become aware of the contradictions, conflicts and questions in play are likely to enter the fray with more clarity, more purpose. (307)

While those definitions address the expansive nature of curriculum and readily apply to post-secondary education, a more categorical definition offers a means to understand what curriculum might look like in writing studies. For that, I turn to William Schubert (2008), who offers the following types of curriculum as commonly found in schools:

- "Intended curriculum" (407), or the curriculum found in curriculum guides, frameworks, outcome statements, syllabi, and textbooks.
- "Taught curriculum" (408), or the actual content with which teachers engage their students in actual classrooms, often in contrast to the "intended curriculum."
- "Experienced curriculum" (408), or the "thoughts, meanings, and feelings of students as they encounter" (409) the intended or taught curriculum.

- "Embodied curriculum" (409), or the ways that students express their learning through imagination and expanded notions of "self."
- "Hidden curriculum" (409), or the cultural and social values that curricular choices and the practices of everyday schooling express, whether notions of social control, power hierarchies, or identities.
- "Tested curriculum" (410), or the knowledge, values, and outcomes that are subject to assessment, whether at the classroom level or on a larger scale, as in standardized assessments.
- "Null curriculum" (410), or the curriculum that is *not* represented in tests and state standards or curriculum frameworks, for example, the paucity of arts and music opportunities in most urban public schools.
- "Outside curriculum" (410), sometimes known as the "extracurriculum" (Gere 1994), or the curricula that students engage with outside of school contexts.

As a way to demonstrate these dimensions, I draw on the example of the First-Year Writing class I last taught (see appendix A for syllabus). Some context: at Northeastern, First-Year Writing is required of all incoming students except for those who place out based on AP or IB scores (typically about 30 percent of the incoming class). It is a one-semester course, offered in both fall and spring, and about sixty to seventy sections run each semester, with a cap of nineteen students (fifteen for sections designated for multilingual writers). Instructors are a mix of non-tenure-track, full-time teaching professors, part-time lecturers, PhD students, and tenure-stream faculty. My particular section had an "experiential education" designation and a relationship with Northeastern's Office of Community Engagement, which meant that I had a dedicated service-learning undergraduate teaching assistant assigned to the course. She handled all the logistics of working with our community partner—a Boston public charter school with a focus on health science careers—where my students worked as writing tutors.

- INTENDED CURRICULUM: Writing Program courses at Northeastern, which include First-Year Writing and an upper-division disciplinary writing course with fourteen different variations, are guided by eleven student learning goals (see http://www.northeastern.edu/writing/student-learning-goals-writing-program/). There is not a common syllabus or textbook, so the clearest intention of curricula for First-Year Writing can be found in those goals. In addition, the course catalog description of First-Year Writing reads as follows:

  First-Year Writing offers students the opportunity to study and practice writing in a workshop setting. Students read a range of texts in order to describe and evaluate the choices writers make and apply that knowledge to their own writing; learn

> to conduct research using primary and secondary sources;
> explore how writing functions in a range of academic, profes-
> sional, and public contexts; and write for various purposes
> and audiences in multiple genres and media. Throughout the
> course, students give and receive feedback, revise their work,
> and reflect on their growth as writers.

Thus, the intended curriculum values *particular student actions* (study, practice, read, evaluate, apply, learn, conduct, explore, give and receive feedback, revise, reflect), *particular contexts for those actions* (workshop setting, academic, professional, and public contexts), *particular rhetorical concepts* (various purposes and audiences), and *particular media* (range of texts, multiple genres and media).

The intended curriculum is also found in my syllabus description, particular to my section:

> Another manifestation of our class theme of **writing, literacy, and educa-
> tion** will be in the research and writing you do over the semester, whether
> exploring your own literacy experiences, making sense of the literacy
> experiences of your classmates, writing opinion pieces on issues specific
> to our theme, or conducting empirical research on your tutoring practices
> at [our high school partner]. These activities are guided by the Writing
> Program Learning Goals (see below), the theme of this course, and the
> evolving needs of the class members.

In this statement, I offer a more explicit idea of the theme of the course and the content of students' writing that will grow out of that theme, as well as their connection to the Writing Program student learn-ing goals, all expressions of the intended curriculum.

- TAUGHT CURRICULUM: As director of the Writing Program at the time I was teaching this course, I would like to think I aligned my *taught curriculum* as tightly as possible with the *intended curriculum.* However, the program's eleven student learning goals are impos-sible to achieve in equal emphasis, as some are more appropriate than others in particular contexts and for particular assignments. In my description of each assignment, I would list the learning goals I felt the assignment responded to, and in the reflection on their writing that students completed, both with each assignment and at the end of the term, I asked them to describe which of the learning goals they felt they addressed. Nonetheless, I cannot say they were all equally addressed, much less met, by each student.

- EXPERIENCED CURRICULUM: As I note above, I did ask students to reflect on the relationship between their writing tasks and the Writing Program student learning goals, and I required ongoing reporting of their experiences tutoring high school students at our community partner site. However, these authorized statements of the experienced curriculum are, of course, only partial, composed in a context in which I, as instructor, controlled the mechanisms of evaluation, that is, grades.

- EMBODIED CURRICULUM: In the weekly informal writing I asked students to do in response to readings or to their service-learning experiences, many would offer descriptions of personal experiences or narrative that were in many ways explorations of identity. Yet these responses were also required, monitored, and sanctioned, surely limiting the extent of students' "personal connection" (Eodice, Geller, and Lerner 2016) to this writing.

- HIDDEN CURRICULUM: As instructor of the course, I likely had many blind spots when it came to what aspects of curriculum were hidden or expressed through my actions, particularly my response to and evaluation of students' writing. My in-class activities featured a great deal of collaborative work, as did some out-of-class assignments, and the service-learning component meant that the undergraduates, a largely privileged though fairly ethnically and racially diverse group, would be working directly with mostly underprivileged students of color in the eleventh and twelfth grades. Thus, aspects of the hidden curriculum potentially included working well with others, exposure to others unlike oneself, and creating reciprocal relationships with community partners. Also, as expressed in my syllabus via policies on attendance, timely submission of work, academic integrity, and classroom interaction, the hidden curriculum of what I value in terms of effort, timeliness, and cooperation is, perhaps, not terribly hidden.

- TESTED CURRICULUM: Students completed three written projects and a final reflective portfolio. While all evaluation criteria for these tasks were generated and negotiated by the class itself (see Inoue 2005), I also graded students on their completion of online discussion prompts, their attendance, and their participation in class activities. The particular behaviors and dispositions I was testing for and thus valuing were additional aspects of the hidden curriculum.

- NULL CURRICULUM: Curricular elements not present were many, as is inevitable in any course, whether as a result of the choices I made as instructor or the parameters as offered through the Writing Program Student Learning Goals. My students were also part of a community in which many peers are also taking First-Year Writing, likely in sections quite different than mine, given the service-learning component. Those sections might have curricular elements, some highly valued by students, some not, that were not present in my section.

- OUTSIDE CURRICULUM: That my students have rich literate lives outside my class is a given, considering the saturation of reading, writing, speaking, listening, and visualizing in mainstream culture. The extent to which my students pursue these activities outside of the sanctions of the institution I do not know for sure—though some research my colleagues and I have done with multilingual undergraduates at Northeastern offers evidence that literate activity, in multiple languages, is commonplace outside of school (see Benda et al. 2018).

This analysis, however incomplete, does attest to the rich and complex nature of curriculum in my First-Year Writing course, far more than might be reflected in a syllabus or in a catalog description alone. These eight dimensions of curriculum are present in every writing studies course to different degrees, and represent particular kinds of knowledge valued (or not) by the institution, by the instructor, and by students.

DESIGNING CURRICULUM

Schubert's (2008) eight dimensions of curriculum represent one way to read existing curricular efforts such as my FYW syllabus. What they don't necessarily reveal are the theoretical and ideological underpinnings of curriculum development. For that I turn to A. V. Kelly's (2004) *The Curriculum: Theory and Practice,* in which he describes the intellectual and political traditions of curriculum design. While Kelly's context is largely primary and secondary schools in the UK, much of what he writes is applicable to education at all levels and thus to higher education in the United States.

Kelly splits curriculum design into the ideas of curriculum as "content and product" versus curriculum as "process and development." The former is marked by the concept that "intrinsic value [is] residing in some way in the knowledge itself rather than in the manner in which the learner approaches it and views it" (2004, 47). This view sees education as "cultural transmission" based on "what is regarded as being best or most valuable, those things which are 'intrinsically worthwhile', among the intellectual and artistic achievements of the society" (49). The danger of this approach is that it "can lead to the imposition on some pupils of a curriculum that is alien to them, which lacks relevance to their lives and to their experience outside the school and can ultimately bring about their alienation from and rejection of the education they are offered" (49–50). Curriculum development as "process and development," on the other hand,

> suggests that our educational purposes should be framed in terms of processes we regard as able and concerned to promote education. Such an approach advises us to select the knowledge-content of our curriculum not by reference to some supposed intrinsic value or its assumed effectiveness in securing certain extrinsic aims or objectives, but in relation to its likely contribution to the development of the pupil. Thus we see these purposes not as goals to be achieved at some later stage in the process but as procedural principles that should guide our practice throughout. (Kelly 2004, 76–77)

This latter definition aligns nicely with writing studies' goals and values for learning and teaching, particularly the view of knowledge as socially constructed and the power of student-centered instruction. However, in practice the development of curriculum in writing studies has features of "content and product" more than "process and development," as I show in the next chapter, a consequence of curriculum's largely hidden role in writing classrooms.

BUT WHAT ABOUT PEDAGOGY?

Before I turn to three recent efforts to describe a potential writing studies curriculum, I return at the end of this chapter to pedagogy. I make this move to ensure that I am not giving pedagogy short shrift or sending the message that writing studies has pedagogy figured out, given its acknowledged presence at all instructional levels. In her book *Pedagogy: Disturbing History, 1819–1929*, Salvatori (1996) notes the movement since the 1970s to infuse definitions of pedagogy with a decided edge: "A need to widen pedagogy's sphere of influence seems to be signaled by the proliferation of such phrases as *liberatory pedagogy*, *critical pedagogy*, and *radical pedagogy*" (1). Salvatori then draws on British film theorist David Lusted to offer a robust definition of pedagogy, one that aligns nicely with curriculum as "process and development" and the larger project of this book:

> Lusted's conceptualization of pedagogy assigned pedagogues an important role. Insofar as pedagogy's function is *not* the transmission of immutable knowledge but instead "the interaction of three agencies—the teacher, the learner and the knowledge they together produce," pedagogues ought to be theorists who rigorously and responsibly practice the theories they espouse . . . This means, among other things, that pedagogues need to begin their investigations "where students are," not in condescension or as a beginning to be quickly left behind, but with a passion and an intellectual curiosity about how students think and the language they use to think, that might lead them to recognize in their students' work telling examples of knowledge formation. (3–4)

What is key here, in terms of the overlap between curriculum and pedagogy, is how both, in order to be effective, need to attend to "the teacher, the learner and the knowledge they together produce." That collaborative knowledge production can readily be found in many college writing classrooms, I would imagine, but in terms of articulating a systematic process, fully informed by a theory of pedagogy *and* curriculum, our field often comes up short.

Salvatori is also concerned with how theory affects the decisions teachers make, writing that "a teacher should be able and willing to interrogate the reasons for his or her adoption of a particular theory and be alert to the possibility that a particular theory and the rigorous practice that enacts it might be ineffectual, or even counterproductive, at certain times or in certain contexts" (1996, 4). I see that statement as applying equally to curriculum. In effect, a curriculum (or a theory or a pedagogy) is only as effective as contexts allow, and space needs to be created for students and teachers to adjust curriculum and pedagogy to their needs and values as learners and teachers rather than to the needs and values of the institution, the state, or some amorphous authority.

An additional concept from the educational literature, specifically the literature on teacher education, helps offer a bridge between pedagogy and curriculum. In a 1986 article, Lee Shulman was critical of the overwhelming focus on pedagogy in teacher education, writing that

> The emphasis is on how teachers manage their classrooms, organize activities, allocate time and turns, structure assignments, ascribe praise and blame, formulate the levels of their questions, plan lessons, and judge general student understanding. What we miss are questions about the *content* of the lessons taught, the questions asked, and the explanations offered. (8)

Shulman, however, was not merely calling for more attention to teachers' mastery of subject matter or content; instead, he introduced the term "pedagogical content knowledge" to capture the additional need for teachers to present their subjects or content areas in "the most useful forms of representation of those ideas, the most powerful analogies, illustrations, examples, explanations, and demonstrations—in a word, the ways of representing and formulating the subject that make it comprehensible to others. Since there are no single most powerful forms of representation, the teacher must have at hand a veritable armamentarium of alternative forms of representation, some of which derive from research whereas others originate in the wisdom of practice" (9).

It's important to note that such knowledge isn't merely on-the-ground strategies of knowledge dissemination. In Shulman's formulation, pedagogical content knowledge also includes "an understanding of what makes the learning of specific topics easy or difficult: the conceptions and preconceptions that students of different ages and backgrounds bring with them to the learning of those most frequently taught topics and lessons. If those preconceptions are misconceptions, which they so often are, teachers need knowledge of the strategies most likely to be fruitful in reorganizing the understanding of learners, because those learners are unlikely to appear before them as blank slates" (9–10). In short, effective teaching requires pedagogical content knowledge that includes knowledge of the subject matter, the learners and what they bring to the classroom, and the context itself, an echo of Salvatori's pedagogical attention to "the teacher, the learner and the knowledge they together produce."

Shulman's concept of "pedagogical content knowledge" has been remarkably robust over the last thirty years in K–12 literature (see Abell 2008; Kleickmann et al. 2017; and Segall 2004), offering a powerful explanation of why those who are subject-matter experts might not automatically be a good fit as teachers. This disconnect is often seen in the "alternative credentialing" programs that hire math and science "experts" at the secondary level and the common experience of a university's top researchers not necessarily being their top teachers (though you never know!). What's most important for the study of curriculum I present in this book is that for learning and teaching to be most effective, all facets need attention: learners, teachers, content, contexts, pedagogy, curriculum. In many of the inquiries that follow, attention has been focused on one aspect or several, but rarely on all, and the result is a perpetuation of the failures of multiple cycles of school reform.

* * *

In the next chapter, I turn to three recent efforts to create writing studies curriculum that emerged in the latest cycle of reform: *The Framework for Success for Postsecondary Writing* (Council of Writing Program Administrators, National Council of Teachers of English, and the National Writing Project 2011), the Writing Program Administrators' "Outcomes Statement" (Council of Writing Program Administrators 2014), and the *Writing about Writing* textbook (and its associated literature) for first-year writing courses (Wardle and Downs 2010). These efforts demonstrate the ways that pedagogical ideas for teaching writing usually crowd out any discussion of curriculum and indicate that when curricula are put forward, whether as a means of disciplinary formation or reformation of first-year writing or both, they tend to be top-down, regulated curricula with a distinct lack of student input. In other words, the creation of opportunities for students to be agentive in and with their writing is rarely a motivating factor. Instead, these efforts at creating curriculum run the risk of becoming momentary fads in the long history of teaching writing in higher education.

2
READY OR NOT, HERE
WE CURRICULUM

As I described in the introduction, my contention in this book is not that we leave curriculum largely unchallenged or in the hands of text-book publishers, school boards (in the K–12 realm), and state legislators (though we usually do); it is that we often do not distinguish between curriculum and pedagogy. That's not to say that the field of writing studies has not addressed curriculum in some ways, largely indirectly, whether via its professional organizations or through attention to what first-year writing classes might look like and do.[1] The efforts at defining curriculum in writing studies that I explore in this chapter—*The Framework for Success in Postsecondary Writing* (Council of Writing Program Administrators, National Council of Teachers of English, and the National Writing Project 2011), the WPA "Outcomes Statement" (Council of Writing Program Administrators 2014), and the *Writing about Writing* textbook (Wardle and Downs 2010)—all contain elements of the eight dimensions of curriculum that I described in the previous chapter, though in their sanctioning by professional organizations and/or publishing companies, they tend to represent the "intended" and often "taught" curricula on the surface and the "hidden" and "null" curricula in their representation. What is most important for the purposes of this book, however, is that while these efforts are often appreciated for their intent to provide instructors with curricular guidance in relatively adaptable form, they ultimately offer models of curriculum in writing studies as hierarchical, static, and removed from the resources and learning "incomes" (Guerra 2008) that all students bring to our classrooms and writing centers. In other words, they position students as consumers of curriculum rather than curriculum makers.[2]

SOWING SEEDS FOR SUCCESS

The Framework for Success in Postsecondary Writing, a collaborative effort between the Council of Writing Program Administrators, the National

DOI: 10.7330/9781607328810.c002

Council of Teachers of English, and the National Writing Project (2011), describes "the rhetorical and twenty-first-century skills as well as habits of mind and experiences that are critical for college success" (1).[3] The well-meaning authors of this report follow a long tradition of similar reports, dating back to Harvard's National Education Association–sponsored *Report of the Committee of Ten* in 1894, claimed at the time to be "the most important educational document ever issued in the United States" (National Educational Association 1894, iii) with its lists of curriculum requirements for high school students who aspired to higher education (Applebee 1974, 32–34). While such efforts and the documents that resulted are bundled up with our hopes for kindergarten-to-college coherence and, ultimately, student learning, the fulfillment of those hopes always seems elusive. After all, the ongoing need to articulate such frameworks for success indicates that current and past efforts might be frameworks for failure.

Despite the ambitions of *Framework for Success*, curriculum and its reform get short shrift. We're told that eight particular "habits of mind" are "essential for success in college writing." Such habits are "intellectual" and "practical," they are "cultivated" like an early spring sowing of seeds, a promise of a fall harvest, a hoped-for abundance, a faith in the vagaries of climate and insects and biology and markets to make that hard work pay off, to produce a bumper crop, to make us forget previous seasons of drought and infestation and disappointment. These eight habits, we are told, are positive ones that students should develop:

Curiosity
Openness
Engagement
Creativity
Persistence
Responsibility
Flexibility
Metacognition

The framework, then, offers a potential blueprint for success in a wide variety of endeavors, not merely postsecondary writing. All it takes is a belief in the power of hope, in the power of the individual to develop positive mental habits to crowd out those negative mental habits, such as avarice, sloth, lust, pride, gluttony, wrath, and envy, which of course are only seven, leaving some question as to just where that eighth positive mental habit might go (or, alternatively, which one might be left out—my money is on openness, the poor cousin to curiosity). This blueprint, of course, is an individual one, placing responsibility for success on the student, not the classroom, not the school system, and just barely with the teacher.[4]

In terms of that teacher, habits are not the only offerings of the *Framework*. Practices are described with the promise that if they are enacted according to the *Framework*, they will offer students experiences in which to develop those habits of mind. These experiences with "writing," "reading," and "critical analysis" are what teachers need to offer; that's their part, to provide "opportunities and guidance." Farmer-teachers thus cultivate a bumper crop of positive habits and weed out the negative ones, bringing to market students ripe for success in college writing classrooms. Of course, some crops are subject to drought or flood or simply rot on the vine. That is expected: it's the justification for sowing more seeds than one could imagine harvesting, it's a planned-for failure that is simply the way of things, the playing of percentages, of relying on the belief that most will be fine, the great majority will turn out well. The misshapen vegetables and shriveled fruits will be plowed under to become fertilizer for next year's crop, the next generation on whom our hopes and dreams depend. Most will succeed with their carefully cultivated habits. As for the failed crop, that is entirely out of our control.

Largely absent in the *Framework* is any mention of curriculum or even the content for students' writing, reading, and thinking. One unfortunate message is that writing classrooms are contentless domains offering mere skills training to instill "habits" and offer "experiences" to a generic student body, not one marked by race or class or gender or sexuality or filled with writerly histories, fears, and goals. Or perhaps writing is a shape-shifting activity, easily fitted to the science or history or business classroom, not a threat to the curricula of those fields, never an intrusion but merely a means to an end.

In my view, the *Framework for Success*, like many of its predecessors, is likely to do little to enact real change. Instead, it is another testament to how process pedagogy has largely succeeded. Meaningful reform of curriculum, however, is much tougher to accomplish, much more subject to federal, state, and local politics, better off avoided lest it spark another round of "culture wars." If anything, evidence abounds that the English curriculum on the K–12 level is undergoing a retrovision as witnessed by two initiatives: (1) the Common Core Standards effort to bring nationwide coherence to public school curricula and student learning outcomes, as well as standardized assessment of those outcomes (see http://commoncorestandards.org); and (2) the well-established state-by-state "accountability" movement marked by high-stakes, standardized competency testing at multiple grade levels, whether the result of the No Child Left Behind Act at the federal level or more long-standing efforts at individual state levels. *The Framework for Success* is meant to speak back to these efforts, but ultimately is largely silent on matters of curriculum and institutional responsibility while offering a familiar voice on pedagogy. It is comforting in a way—our professional organizations are doing *something* about the latest perceived literacy crisis and that something represents what we know about best pedagogical practices—but such efforts potentially do little to smooth the transition from high school to college writing, much less make high school writing engaging and meaningful.

One nod to curriculum does appear at the very end of the "Context" statement for the *Framework*: "Standardized writing curricula or assessment instruments that emphasize formulaic writing for nonauthentic audiences will not reinforce the habits of mind and the experiences necessary for success as students encounter the writing demands of postsecondary education" (Council of Writing Program Administrators, National Council of Teachers of English, and the National Writing Project 2011, 3). Of course, curricula "that emphasize formulaic writing for nonauthentic audiences" coexisting with the kind of pedagogical practices called for in the *Framework* are what students often experience. Our expertise is asserted. Pedagogy is our thing. Standardized or not, curriculum seems out of our control, particularly for the current generation of adjunct writing instructors, rushing from one class to the next, truly concerned about their students' learning but with few means to influence curricular decision making. For the professional organizations that potentially have such influence, cultivating habits of mind does not exactly plant seeds of change. It is a specialty crop, the arugula of education reform, savored by a small elite but offering little to feed the vast majority of hungry students who bear the brunt of the responsibility if they are not successful.

While *The Framework for Success* is intended to describe the "habits" that students ideally would bring to the college writing classroom, the Writing Program Administrators' "Outcomes Statement" (WPA-OS) is intended to offer a framework for what students should take away from those classroom experiences. I next turn to that effort.

OUTCOMES, NOT INCOMES

I start this section with a standard academic rhetorical move—yes, but. First the yeses:

- Yes, the WPA-OS is a conscious and deliberate effort to construct curriculum, particularly for college-level first-year writing.
- Yes, the WPA-OS is admirable for its process of development: a collaborative, multi-year effort by well-meaning professionals in writing studies.
- Yes, the WPA-OS is an attempt to offer coherent "learning outcomes" to first-year writing classes (and writing classes beyond the first year) across the United States (and potentially abroad; see Thomas 2013).
- Yes, the WPA-OS is a way to determine for ourselves (assuming some collective "our" exists) what might occur in first-year writing classes rather than have that curriculum determined by "standards" imposed by government and/or administrative functionaries.
- Yes, the intent of the WPA-OS is for writing instructors to have flexibility and freedom in the ways they might structure first-year writing classes so that students might achieve those outcomes.
- Yes, the WPA-OS is framed by a good deal of current research and theory on writing in higher education, that is, disciplinary knowledge from writing studies.

Now the buts:

- But the WPA-OS takes an extremely narrow view of curriculum, largely outcomes = intended curriculum, with some nod toward the taught curriculum.
- But the WPA-OS takes a view of curriculum as fixed, stable, and delivered, rather than contingent and permeable or devoted to "process and development."
- But the WPA-OS does not mention students' roles in determining their fates/outcomes but instead offers strategies for "faculty in all program and departments" to help students achieve outcomes.
- But the WPA-OS does not take into account student learning/ development, instead seeing an outcome as a onetime goal.
- But the WPA-OS's attempt to codify outcomes/curriculum in first-year writing runs the risk of becoming a regulatory structure, imposed upon teachers and students.

Some background on the WPA-OS: this effort to define, frame, and "articulate a general curricular framework for first-year writing" (Yancey 2001, 321) began in 1996 when it was first taken up on the Writing Program Administration listserv, WPA-L, and then further shaped at workshops and discussion at professional conferences and via its own dedicated online discussion. The result, released in 2000, was sponsored and endorsed by the Council of Writing Program Administrators, posted on that organization's website, and published in its journal, *WPA: Writing Program Administration* (Yancey 2001, 322).

It was then introduced to a potentially wider audience in *College English* in 2001. A revised version of the WPA-OS was released in 2008, and the latest version (3.0) came out in 2014 (see http://www.wpacouncil.org /positions/outcomes.html). The later versions are more expansive than the original, particularly when it comes to students composing in multimodal modes and developing genre knowledge. The history, application, and implications of the WPA-OS have also been the subject of two book-length collections: *The Outcomes Book: Debate and Consensus After the WPA Outcomes Statement* (Harrington et al. 2005) and *The WPA Outcomes Statement—A Decade Later* (Behm et al. 2013b). Overall, with barely any dissent,[5] the WPA-OS has dominated professional and local conversations when it comes to the long-vexing question of what first-year writing should be about and for whom. As Kathleen Blake Yancey described in 2001,

> The Outcomes Statement is a curricular document that speaks to the common expectations, for students, of first-year composition programs in the United States at the beginning of the 21st century. Central to the document is the belief that in articulating those expectations and locating them more generally, we help students meet them, and we help assure that the conditions for meeting them are realized. (323)

Yes, but.

My issues with the WPA-OS are several, outlined in my "buts" above. Here I want to focus specifically on three areas: (1) the notion of the WPA-OS as "delivered curriculum" and thus fundamentally representing a transmission model of student learning; (2) the absence of the resources and goals that all students bring to their learning in the WPA-OS, thus fundamentally representing a deficit, nondevelopmental model of student learning; (3) the ways that the WPA-OS is, by its nature, a-contextual, thus fundamentally blind when it comes to anyone's beliefs as to why first-year writing might or might not be important or worth teaching.

SIT AND DELIVER: The 2014 version of the WPA-OS describes student learning outcomes—what all students should be able to know and do by the end of first-year writing—in the categories of "rhetorical knowledge," "critical thinking, reading, and composing," "processes," and "knowledge of conventions." It does not dictate what students should write about or what forms that writing might take, but instead states that "writers develop rhetorical knowledge by negotiating purpose, audience, context, and conventions as they compose a variety of texts for different situations." In Harrington's (2005) words, "The Outcomes Statement does not prescribe curriculum; rather, it encourages conversation about curriculum" (xvii).

What is also important in the genesis of the WPA-OS and its originators' belief that it is not prescriptive is that the WPA-OS was meant to
counter the idea of "standards" in first-year writing. Ericsson (2005)
recounts in her history of the document that

> discussion of the Outcomes Statement began the same month (March
> 1996) that the NCTE/IRA Standards for the English Language Arts
> (National Council 1996) were published. Although the NCTE/IRA stan-
> dards and the outcomes were not directly related in the online discussions
> that spawned the Outcomes Statement, participants in the Outcomes
> Statement discussion were keenly aware of the standards movement and
> the troubled NCTE/IRA project . . . Those working on the Outcomes
> Statement were also aware of the *standards creep* that was taking place. The
> nationwide move towards standards-based education that began in the
> early 1980s with the *Nation at Risk* report had moved steadily up through
> the educational echelons and was making its way into higher education.
> Those involved in the Outcomes Statement movement realized that in
> short order, first-year composition would be a target of the standards
> movement. Preventing the first-year course from being defined by those
> outside of the discipline was one of the prime motivators of the Outcomes
> Statement. (115)

Yancey (2005) contributes to this discourse of the WPA-OS as an anti-
standards effort in her essay in *The Outcomes Book*, noting that "while outcomes articulate the curriculum, they do not specify *how well* students
should know or understand or do what the curriculum intends" (21).
Later in her chapter, she adds the following: "It seems increasingly clear
to me that outcomes assessment is, ironically, an exercise in curriculum
much more than in assessment. It is through articulating our expectations
that we create outcomes, that we then have these to share with students,
that we begin to think not of what's barely doable, but of what's visionary
for our students—and for ourselves" (23). This notion of the WPA-OS as
"shared" is taken up by Hokanson's contribution to the 2005 collection as
he "shares" Alverno College's experience adopting the WPA-OS:

> Well-crafted outcomes linked to the curriculum constitute a common lan-
> guage that clarifies what we mean by effective performance. This shared
> frame of reference benefits everyone involved in the learning process: for
> students, clearly defined outcomes help promote understanding of course
> expectations and their own performance and development over time;
> for faculty, outcomes not only provide a basis for coherent curriculum
> design and informed pedagogy but also promote a continuing conversa-
> tion within and across the disciplines about our goals and expectations as
> educators; and, of course outcomes provide a means by which faculty and
> administrators can assess the progress of their program toward meeting
> institutional goals—and a means of expressing that progress in terms that
> are understandable to various publics. (150–51).

Yes, but.

Now, I'm fairly sure the WPA-OS "collective" did not see its work as canonical or limiting the range of "acceptable" knowledge to be taken up in first-year writing and beyond. Nevertheless, the function of an Outcomes Statement is to do just that—limit what might be acceptable knowledge, offer an extrinsically determined set of knowledge claims (despite invitations for local conversations sparked by the WPA-OS), and succumb to a view of curriculum as transmitted rather than constructed. In this way the WPA-OS is consistent with the very "standards" movements that the originators decry—it might not be describing what particular standards are, but it certainly does prescribe what the knowledge domains of first-year writing should be and thus a belief that those domains are fixed, essential, and canonical.

A CONSPICUOUS ABSENCE: My second major issue with the WPA-OS is the lack of consideration of students' "incomes" (Guerra 2008) when it comes to first-year writing or any other writing course. Guerra's remarks about the need for high schools and colleges to focus on the resources students bring to their learning are particularly appropriate: "Educational institutions are focusing almost exclusively on *learning outcomes* and generally ignoring *learning incomes*—i.e., what students bring with them when they come to school" (296).

Two passages from the 2013 WPA-OS edited collection are particularly noteworthy for their attempt to point to the constructed nature of student learning outcomes, but students themselves are nowhere to be found:

> What the WPA OS fosters . . . is the value of a bottom-up, generative approach that centers on collaboration requiring the involvement of (and investment by) a large group of stakeholders, ranging from program directors to university librarians, from full-time lecturers and part-time adjunct faculty to graduate teaching assistants. (Behm et al. 2013a, xiii)

> For many courses, the subject or theme, as well as writing topics, used in first-year composition are determined by the instructor. While many writing programs have a set of goals, and perhaps a pre-determined textbook, ultimately it is the teacher's responsibility to develop writing assignments that meet course and programmatic outcomes. With the WPA OS in mind, teachers continue to have the same flexibility and freedom regarding classroom content—which topics to cover and what types of documents students should produce. (Rankins-Robertson 2013, 59)

That students are absent from the list of "stakeholders" and that teachers get "flexibility and freedom" while students are producing "documents" based on teacher-chosen "topics" seems a pretty retro-vision of what any writing class might look like. In the 2005 collection, among the "dissenting" voices is Peter Elbow, who makes note of this absence of student input, writing that "decisions about how to frame or articulate knowledge are always deployments of power. The Outcomes Statement as we now have it constitutes an insistence on retaining power to ourselves as professional experts—and refusing to invite power and participation by the student learner *or* the outside world. I'd call it professionalism in the bad sense" (2005, 186). The WPA-OS, then, reinforces a view of students as passive receptacles of writing and rhetorical knowledge, not active, agentive creators of meaningful writing (Eodice, Geller, and Lerner, 2016).

This absence of students' participation in determining outcomes is clear in the WPA-OS itself. The introduction to the 2014 version notes that the OS "describes the writing knowledge, practices, and attitudes that undergraduate students develop in first-year composition." However, there's no mention of students' roles in determining their fates/outcomes; the statement instead offers strategies for "faculty in all program and departments" to help students achieve outcomes. Thus, the responsibility is largely on students for "meeting the outcomes," not exactly letting instructors or institutions off the hook, but the burden of performance rests with students, a model of instruction that largely focuses on teaching rather than learning.

Along these lines, the absence of developmental thinking in the WPA-OS is quite striking. In the 2005 edited collection, Haswell (2005b) is offered an opportunity to weigh in on this absence, but his admonitions were certainly never taken up in subsequent versions of the WPA-OS. I give more attention to what the process of curriculum building in writing studies might ideally look like in chapter 8, but my point here is that the WPA-OS is not informed by research and theory on student development as learners, a significant omission.

Abolish or polish: Given the a-contextual nature of the WPA-OS and the imprimatur supplied by its professional association sponsor, the WPA-OS becomes reified and allows little room when it comes to teacher beliefs for what should take place in first-year writing or why the course might or might not be important and worth teaching. Chris Gallagher (2012) points to this reification in his critique of the WPA-OS:

> In many programs, outcomes become isolated, over time, from the ongoing activities of teachers and students. Whether administrators and faculty begin with great enthusiasm or great skepticism (or, most likely, a mix), outcomes, once expressed, often stay in place for years, even as programs change. Teachers may dutifully reproduce those outcomes on a syllabus or assignment, and students may dutifully provide evidence that they've

achieved them in their work products, but rarely do the outcomes become a meaningful and intimate part of teachers' and students' experiences. In these programs, outcomes—whether the hard-won result of intense consensus building or an administrative hand-me-down—tend to become enshrined in the bureaucratic machinery. (45)

Given the labor situation in U.S. colleges and universities and the dependence on contingent, part-time instructors to teach required writing, for those institutions that adopt the WPA-OS on its face, there is an even greater danger of being seen as promoting a top-down mandate, not an organically generated, locally owned effort.

That first-year writing itself is a part of the "bureaucratic machinery" is clear from its long history in U.S. higher education, a story that has been documented by many scholars (e.g., Connors 1997; Crowley 1998; and Miller 1993). Concurrent with the requirement have been calls to abolish it altogether, whether because of its labor practices, its position in the university as a "service" course, or its inevitable enforcement of dominant culture literacy practices (see Brooks 2002 for a summary of these arguments). Whatever the position, these conversations around the nature, purpose, and need for first-year writing are pretty well steamrolled once the WPA-OS is in place. It becomes a regulatory, top-down mandate: curriculum as "product" and students and teachers as consumers of that product.

To be clear, I am not necessarily advocating that we abolish the first-year writing requirement (though I embrace many of the merits of that position) but that we have the space in our institutions for conversation about the value of the requirement. As I will repeat throughout this book, curriculum is a representation of values, and the values historically conveyed by mandated writing curricula are that students represent deficits to be corrected, vessels to be filled with the time-tested knowledge of the field, strangers in the strange land of higher education.

Certainly, the values built into the WPA-OS speak to more mature visions of who students are and what they might do, but they still do not leave room for teacher and student agency to determine those values.

A CURRICULAR PEDAGOGICAL APPROACH:
WRITING ABOUT WRITING (WAW) IN FYW

A few semesters ago, I decided to use Elizabeth Wardle and Doug Downs's *Writing about Writing* (2010, 2014, 2016) in my first-year writing class. At the end of the first class meeting, after I explained to my students what the approach would be, two students came up to me. "Do any sections use a writing-about-reading approach?" one asked, with the other nodding. "I think I'd rather do that."

When it comes to articulating curriculum in first-year writing, writing about writing (or WAW) is a relatively recent effort. Wardle and Downs first introduced the concept in a 2007 *College Composition and Communication* article, describing their approach as a counter to "acting as if writing is a basic, universal skill" and instead "acting as if writing studies is a discipline with content knowledge to which students should be introduced, thereby changing their understandings about writing and thus changing the ways they write" (553). Here's what that approach looks like in their 2007 description:

> We propose a radically reimagined [first-year writing] as an Introduction to Writing Studies . . . The course includes many of the same activities as current [first-year writing] courses: researching, reading, and writing arguments. However, the course content explores reading and writing: How does writing work? How do people use writing? What are the problems related to writing and reading and how can they be solved? Students read writing research, conduct reading and writing auto-ethnographies, identify writing-related problems that interest them, write reviews of existing literature on their chosen problems, and conduct their own primary research, which they report both orally and in writing. (558)

The intended curriculum of this course is aligned with the research questions that dominate the field of writing studies, offering a comfort zone for writing instructors, who presumably are scholars in the field: "When the course content is writing studies, writing instructors are concretely enabled to fill that expert reader role. This change directly contravenes the typical assumption that first-year writing can be about anything, that somehow the content is irrelevant to an instructor's ability to respond to writing" (559). Along these lines, tapping into teacher expertise has the potential to alter the labor landscape of first-year writing, according to Downs and Wardle (2007):

> Instructors must be educated in writing studies to teach the curriculum we suggest, and a significant portion of the national corps of college writing instructors do not have appropriate training to do so. In this sense, ours is a truth-telling course; it forefronts the field's current labor practices and requires that we ask how [first-year writing] students are currently being served by writing instructors who *couldn't* teach a writing studies pedagogy. (575)

There's a lot to like in the WAW approach. WAW's agenda of articulating and thus owning disciplinary content seems to be an important means of establishing a visible writing studies curriculum, an essential component of disciplinary status. And I believe that WAW's focus on undergraduates producing actual research rather than merely being consumers of published research studies is to be applauded. If anything, the focus on how writing works in students' worlds—past, current, and future—is consistent with literacy studies more generally and is aligned with the goals I've had as a writing instructor for nearly thirty years. But considering WAW as a *curriculum* means recognizing many of its shortcomings. I focus on three: (1) the confusing identification of WAW as pedagogical or curricular or both; (2) the danger of WAW as yet another regulatory structure imposed on students from on high; (3) the logic of WAW leading to disciplinary status and transformation of labor practices.

CURRICULUM OR PEDAGOGY OR . . . ? As I hope I've made clear, it's essential that writing studies recognizes what it means by "curriculum"; identifying and defining that term is the first step toward achieving curricular goals. One of the more frustrating (well, for me, at least) aspects of the literature surrounding WAW are the ways that the terms "curriculum" and "pedagogy" get conflated. In their 2007 *CCC* article, Downs and Wardle kick off this trend: "Part of our purpose here is to insist on deep disciplinary implications of [first-year writing] pedagogy; a pedagogical move whose intention is to help resituate an entire field within the academy demonstrates that pedagogy has impact beyond the daily teaching to-do list" (554). Elsewhere in that article, they describe WAW as a "more pedagogically successful alternative" (554) and an "introductory pedagogy" (554). In a 2012 book chapter, Downs and Wardle again refer to WAW as a "pedagogy" and in that essay offer to "explore this 'writing-about-writing' (WAW) pedagogy as an area of cutting-edge pedagogical research in composition studies" (123). Yet in these two works and elsewhere, together and separately, Downs and Wardle also refer to WAW as a "curriculum," whether it's a 2007 reference to teaching "the curriculum we suggest" (575); Downs's (2010) title for his WPA-CompPile research bibliography, "Writing-about-Writing Curricula: Origins, Theories, and Initial Field-Tests"; or Downs and Wardle's 2012 offering of "curriculum descriptions: Ways of writing-about writing" (137). In that 2012 book chapter, Downs and Wardle move from "pedagogies" to "curricula" in the course of a paragraph, noting that "while there is common ground across WAW *pedagogies*, there is also substantial variation . . . The most obvious distinction among WAW *curricula* is that they may focus on writing and literacy from distinctly different angles" (139; emphasis added). Later in that chapter, they conflate a whole bunch of terms: "Proponents of WAW pedagogies enact curricula that suggest it is possible for students to write *about* a content for which the teacher is a qualified reader and which stresses rather than detracts from the writing-related knowledge that should be the focus of a writing course" (143): *pedagogies, curricula, content, knowledge,* all in one sentence!

I think it's pretty clear that WAW represents an intended curriculum as it defines the content of and rationale for a first-year writing course (i.e., what students will be writing about, how, and why) and the goals for student learning. It does not call for pedagogical approaches that would push most first-year writing instructors out of their comfort zones: process pedagogies still abide. And as an identified curriculum, the need is to view WAW through the lens of curriculum theory. What's the "null" curriculum, or what's left out in a WAW approach? What's the "hidden" curriculum in a WAW classroom? How might WAW represent the idea of curriculum and product delivered to students rather than process co-constructed with students?

And what might research on the effectiveness of WAW look like?

I am not calling for a rejection of WAW, only a more critical view than has been taken so far. WAW has reached the level of "movement" (Downs, quoted in McMillan 2011) with a great deal of associated activity: a Conference on College Composition and Communication special-interest group (now a standing group), a dedicated listserv, the Writing-about-Writing Network, and a Ning (Downs and Wardle 2012, 130). There's a sense of "true-believer-ism" among its advocates, if not a kind of religious zeal, represented by McMillan's 2011 review of the initial edition of Downs and Wardle's WAW textbook: "For those, like me, who have already converted to WAW but have been cobbling together their own readers or making do with a composition text that is 'good enough'—well, I'm sure they are happy about the new choice" (2).

That textbook is in its third edition at the time of this writing, a sure sign that the WAW curriculum has been imbedded in the FYW landscape.

What's most troubling to me about this "movement" is its expansion without concomitant scrutiny, both in terms of defining it as curricular and in subjecting it to rigorous assessment. In curriculum design, assessment bridges the gap between the "intended" curriculum and the "achieved" curriculum (Black 2000). While he refers to K–12 contexts in the UK, Black's description of what assessment of the achieved curriculum might entail applies equally well to an assessment of WAW: "Deeper understanding [of the curriculum] is achieved if pupils can talk about the meaning of what they have done, but such achievement can only be evaluated by listening to pupils' talk and looking at what they produce, be this in writing or through other artifacts, with holistic styles of summative assessment appropriate to judgment of enriched understanding and development of capacity to learn in complex contexts" (21). Perhaps recognizing WAW as curricular will lead to these sorts of assessment efforts, to know in depth and across multiple contexts how the "movement" has translated into student learning.

WAW AS CURRICULUM PRODUCT: Along with the dangers of uncritical adoption of WAW by true believers are that ways that it easily becomes yet another regulatory structure foisted upon students as *consumers* of curriculum. In a response to Downs and Wardle's 2007 debut of WAW, Miles et al. (2008) point to the danger of WAW as offering a set definition of the discipline of writing studies:

> Rather than telling students what Writing Studies is, we now have an opportunity to learn from our students what it might be. Rather than codify, canonize, and normalize a narrow band of one definition for what Writing Studies is (or should be), choose instead a more post disciplinary route: a local and organic field of study with rhetorical habits mind, a robust and intellectually driven frame for a vertical curriculum, but with no fixed end-product or telos. We are adamantly not interested in merely reproducing ourselves in our students, turning them into mini-scholars with unpolished papers. There is more, and more important, work to do. Thus, our teaching can be—and is—informed by our deep knowledge of the field without limiting the core to first-year writing or *any* single course. (510)

Wardle's (2008) published response to this charge was to deny that her and Downs's intent was to "define 'writing studies'" (178) via the curriculum of WAW.

Nevertheless, articles describing WAW take a uniform stance of students as recipients of delivered curriculum, not as co-constructors. For example, Wardle and Downs (2013) write that WAW has a particular relationship to what's "known" in writing studies and what students might do with that knowledge: "We see our field as having both declarative and procedural knowledge about writing that can and should be conveyed directly to students, so that they are empowered by knowing about the nature and workings of the activity itself and can act from their knowledge instead of having writing done *to* them" (2). It's difficult to see "conveying of knowledge" as anything but a belief in a transmission model of teaching, no matter the claims of "empowerment." Downs and Wardle take up this possibility in their 2007 introduction of WAW, noting that "to center the course on student writing and avoid merely banking information, students discuss, write about, and test every reading in light of their own experiences; they discuss why they are reading a piece and how it might influence their understanding of writing" (561). That this process (or, more accurately, this pedagogy) starts with "merely banking" and then offers students opportunities to validate that transmitted knowledge is better than no opportunities at all. But without the kinds of assessment I called for earlier or a commitment to a developmental framework that I described in relation to the WPA-OS, it's still banking, though perhaps with expanded hours.

IT'S THE LABOR, STUPID: The argument that WAW will somehow transform both labor practices and the disciplinary status of writing studies is the one that I find most difficult to accept. In terms of labor, Wardle and Downs (2013) make the following point: "A course that teaches writing studies content requires prepared and trained teachers—preparation and training that cannot be demanded of low-paid, disrespected, last-minute hires" (1).[6] It's difficult for me to imagine this mechanism, particularly as I would argue that any first-year writing course, no matter the curriculum, requires "prepared and trained teachers" if we want the course to be effective. The dependence on lower-paid, contingent faculty to teach writing courses is due to many factors. While I am sympathetic and have experienced firsthand as a WPA the wrongheaded and entrenched notion that "anyone can teach writing," I still don't see the presence of a "teacher-proof" curriculum a contributing factor to current labor practices. Labor economists Dell Champlin and Janet Knoedler (2016) point out that the hiring of contingent faculty in higher education is part of a larger long-term trend of hiring contingent labor in the U.S. work force, as well as the growth of online distance education and the transformation of the purpose of a college degree toward a professional career (as opposed to intellectual or civic goals). That there's a direct relationship between curriculum and hiring practices is dubious, particularly when one looks at hiring practices across all disciplines, including those with long-established and relatively stable content areas.

This logic of this argument—essentially, that this curriculum requires expertise that part-timers and adjuncts don't have; therefore, we won't hire them—also ignores the large presence of graduate students teaching first-year writing and the role of first-year writing as a particular kind of mentoring space. One might argue that such mentoring for graduate students in writing studies will be more powerful with a WAW curriculum, but graduate-student labor usually draws from the range of graduate English programs, including creative writing, professional and technical communication, film study, literature, and digital humanities, as well as rhetoric and composition. This variety of graduate students will have varying levels of commitment to writing studies and its enduring questions. The likely outcome is not that WAW will narrow the teaching cadre to those with writing studies expertise, but that the wide range of writing instructors will be handed a ready-made WAW curriculum, complete with textbook and instructors' guide (as is included in the second edition of *Writing about Writing*), and be held accountable for how faithfully they stick to the plan. Once again, the curriculum is more regulatory than liberatory, both for instructors and students.

Finally, the logic that establishing a writing studies curriculum in first-year writing will lead to disciplinary recognition and respectability doesn't quite work for me. Downs and Wardle describe this argument in their 2007 article: "[The WAW-based course] has the added benefit of educating first-year students, adjuncts, and graduate students about the existence and content of the writing studies field. Over time, as these groups move on to other disciplines, professions, and administrative positions, their knowledge about our field may be of assistance in creating more writing studies majors. At the very least, educating the public about our discipline in this way should result in a more widespread understanding and awareness of its existence, focus, and research findings" (578). Well, maybe, but having taught this required course for nearly thirty years now, I'm hard pressed to see first-year students coming to a disciplinary understanding of writing studies any more than any other required course—particularly for the many students who do not become writing studies majors or where that possibility, such as at my own institution, does not exist. Truthfully, my English department colleagues and I spend a lot of time imagining that one killer first-year course that not only generates lots of income for the college because it puts fannies in seats but also acts as a recruiting tool for would-be English majors. Such hopes, of course, mostly reveal our ignorance about the ways students choose majors. If anything, this idea of WAW's not-so-hidden agenda as a disciplinary recruitment tool for cultivating undergraduate writing majors seems likely to create ill will in a university structure where departments without required or core classes do not always look favorably on departments who do have such classes, largely because of the way students' enrollments equate to funding streams.

As far as WAW leading to disciplinary status, I am in support of identifying a writing studies curriculum or at least a well-designed process for building that curriculum. To focus that curriculum primarily on first-year writing and then to have it be determined largely *for* students rather than *with* students does not, however, represent an effort for which I can advocate.

FROM HABITS TO OUTCOMES TO CURRICULA
TO THRESHOLD CONCEPTS

The latest effort to determine what knowledge counts in writing studies and how best to turn that knowledge into curriculum can be found in the idea of "threshold concepts."[7] These represent "concepts critical for continued learning and participation in an area or within a community of practice" (Adler-Kassner and Wardle 2015, 2), or, I would add, a discipline.[8] It's too soon to know if this approach will offer a kind of disciplinary stability and productive work that the three efforts I describe in this chapter intend. Already, there's an edited collection (Adler-Kassner and Wardle 2015) and a "classroom edition" of that collection (Adler-Kassner and Wardle 2016), though Adler-Kassner and Wardle (2015) warn in the introduction to the collection that "these threshold concepts should in no way, shape, or form be used as a checklist—for the development of curriculum, for instance, or to check students' learning" (8). Still, curriculum happens, particularly curriculum with the imprimatur of what's essential to know in a field.

The three highly visible efforts at determining curriculum in writing studies that I have described in this chapter represent particular sites of inquiry. In the chapters that follow, my sites of inquiry range away from first-year writing in college and toward a variety of times and places in which curriculum—or its absence—plays a major role. In the next chapter, I turn to an experiential inquiry, focusing on the eight years I spent as a part-time adjunct writing instructor when the opportunities to play a role in the development of curriculum were unfortunately rare, and thus it was even rarer for my students to co-construct that curriculum.

NOTES

1. See Dedek (2016, ch. 1) for a history of writing studies' attempts to define "curriculum."

2. For this distinction between students as creators versus consumers of curriculum, I'm indebted to Michael Dedek, whose dissertation ("Practicing Change: Curricular Innovation and Change in Writing Programs") smartly explored the presence of curriculum in composition studies.

3. *The Framework for Success* is also reprinted in full in the July 2012 issue of *College English*, which offers a "symposium" on the document, including a statement on its creation and a series of five brief responses. Of those responses, my scorecard reads three largely against (McComiskey; Severino; Summerfield and Anderson), one fairly neutral (Hansen), and one in favor (Sullivan). See also Adler-Kassner 2012 for support of the *Framework* as an articulation of writing studies' beliefs about high school students' readiness for college writing.

4. See Carillo 2017 for a critique of composition studies' current drift toward investigating individual cognition, often at the expense of understanding the larger social context.

5. Chris Gallagher's 2012 "The Trouble with Outcomes" being pretty much the only dissenting opinion while Beaufort, also in 2012, pointed out some limits of the WPA-OS in not fully considering students' transfer of their writing knowledge.

6. In their preface to the second edition of *Writing about Writing* (2014) Wardle and Downs note that "we have designed the book to be as accessible as possible to composition instructors with a wide range of experience, including new graduate students and very busy adjuncts" (x). While likely a publisher's conceit, this statement does reveal the ways the curriculum is shaped by available labor rather than vice versa.

7. The second edition of *Writing about Writing* (Wardle and Downs 2014) is structured around five threshold concepts.

8. An anonymous reviewer of an earlier draft of this book made the smart point that writing studies' embrace of "genre," perhaps best known in Miller's (1984) conception of "genre as social action," represents another manifestation of curriculum particularly prevalent in first-year writing classrooms. However, this trend, given the reliance on part-time adjuncts who are handed ready-made curricula, is subject to becoming largely regulatory structures for writing (akin to the current-traditional "march through the modes") rather than opportunities for student knowledge construction.

PART 2

Experiential Inquiries

3

LEARNING TO TEACH AS A FREEWAY FLYER

Here's my teacher's history in a somewhat large nutshell: In 1986, I enrolled in a creative writing MA English program at San Jose State University in San Jose, California, with the intention of continuing the fiction-writing career I felt I had already committed myself to as an undergraduate. An additional incentive was that I might live off of student loans! And, I figured, if the fiction-writing thing didn't work out, I could always teach (while not having a clue as to what kind of preparation and credentialing that would entail). My first semester at SJSU, I took Practical Approaches to Composition, taught by Hans Guth, and this course was truly a watershed moment in my career. Guth, a veteran and well-respected member of his field at that point, treated us all—experienced or not—as composition and rhetoric colleagues, and that class sparked my interest in composition and rhetoric as a field of study, as well as a realization that teaching might offer the creative outlet and opportunity to make a social contribution that had an extremely slim chance of happening in my pursuit of a career as a fiction writer.

The next year, I enrolled in a program at SJSU to earn a high school English teaching credential simultaneous with my MA and embarked on a semester of intensive study and two semesters of student teaching. That education program was focused on liberatory pedagogy; we read Paolo Freire (1968), Henry Giroux (1988), and Ira Shor (1986), among others, focusing on critiques of public schooling and the role of literacy as a tool of both oppression and of liberation. It all resonated strongly with my interests and goals, and by the time I had graduated in 1989 and started teaching college-level writing classes that fall, I was committed to a career as a writing teacher intending to use writing to transform students' lives, if not civic society itself.

The first eight of those years (1989 to 1997), I was a part-time instructor and taught thirty-eight separate sections of writing classes, covering thirteen colleges in three states. Those classes ranged from lowest-level developmental writing to first-year writing to British and American

DOI: 10.7330/9781607328810.c003

literature to creative writing to business writing to film studies. My students included learning-disabled adults, eighteen-year-olds fresh out of high school, active military and military veterans, adults returning to or starting college many years after high school, government employees, Ford automotive technicians, and nuclear power plant employees. I also tutored writing one-to-one during that time, whether at university writing centers or for private tutoring services. From 1992 to 1996, I was also a full-time doctoral student, picking up writing classes and writing tutoring to augment my wife's salary as a new assistant professor.

I look back on this period with both a sense of disbelief that I could handle the load of teaching as many as seven courses per semester (which I did not do particularly well) and a feeling of gratitude that I was able to hone my craft in a wide variety of contexts and with a wide range of students. That's not to say that I endorse this labor model. Hiring the least experienced to teach one of the most important classes in a student's college career is surely misguided, as composition scholars have continually pointed out (e.g., Connors 1997; Crowley 1998). That I had the opportunity to learn at the expense of my students' learning is certainly nothing to be proud of. And as I noted in the introduction to this book, my opportunities to shape curriculum and to engage with students to co-construct curriculum were essentially nil. In my application to join the 1991 San Jose–Area Writing Project Summer Institute, I described this tension:

> In the community colleges where I teach, much of the instruction is very traditional. Classrooms are dutifully lined up in rows, students passively listening to lecture. Many of the writing teachers are most concerned with their students' inability to write within conventional expectations: the five-paragraph structure with cause-effect reasoning, a compare/contrast essay, a process paragraph. Many have stopped having their students write narrative essays because they weren't "academic" enough and because students were dwelling "too much on personal experience." My approach, however, has been to use writing in order for my students to come to an understanding of their own experience, to become active rather than passive participants in their own lives.

Needless to say, I was an idealist and not a little naïve. Nearly thirty years, scores of classes, and likely over a thousand students later, I'm certainly less naïve, perhaps somewhat cynical, but still reasonably idealistic, if that's possible. I still see the power of literacy as a means of transformation, whether for individual students or the larger public good. But I have also seen—and perhaps practiced—literacy and schooling as a means of social control. It is this tension that I explore in this book through the lens of curriculum, one highly visible in K–12 settings, much less so in college writing classrooms, but certainly essential to recognize and, if possible, reform.

I don't know if my nearly thirty years as a writing teacher are typical or anomalous. My current colleagues and I do not spend a lot of time sharing teacher histories, or perhaps it's just that I'm reluctant to share my story, assuming that it's quite different from the undergraduate-degree-to-PhD-program-to-tenure-track-position path of many of my tenure-stream faculty colleagues. Then again, my assumption that this path is the norm for my colleagues—without me knowing for sure—likely says more about my insecurities than it does about the realities of my colleagues' teaching histories. We are all in extremely privileged positions as tenure-stream faculty in an English department in a private research I institution. Perhaps that privilege itself comes with a certain amount of insecurity, a variant of "imposter syndrome."

As I read back through the notes and journals that I kept regularly during the first several years of my teaching, that insecurity seems to be a consistent presence. It makes these materials difficult to read; it is difficult to relive how I constantly worried about how well I was doing, how my students were doing, how I was not getting enough sleep or exercise or leisure time or returning graded papers back to students in a timely manner. I was kind of a mess.

At the same time, I had a consistent commitment to my students' learning, to countering their dissatisfaction with schooling and writing, particularly my developmental writing students. I was asserting a particular curriculum—one that I often assumed my students would share, but I encountered inevitable resistance when they did not. To be student-centered, after all, is to assert a particular view of how students best learn, how classrooms and schools should be organized, what teachers should and should not do. It's no less an assertion of curriculum than were I to lecture and then test students' recall of those lectures through multiple-choice examinations. I happen to believe—and a significant amount of research supports those beliefs (e.g., National Research Council 2000) that students best learn, particularly in writing classes, through student-centered approaches. But as I have noted previously, curriculum is an assertion of values, and asserting is what I was doing. Those values were a result of my own experiences as a student and as a writer, my sense of social justice and the inequities of current schooling, my sense of right and wrong. All teachers come to their work with these value sets, asserted through the choices they make with and to students. I don't mean to claim my values should prevail here, only that the curriculum I created for my students—whether "intended," "taught," or "hidden" (Schubert 2008)—was a driving force, just as it is in any writing classroom.

In this chapter, I take a narrative approach to exploring curriculum, drawing from my writing—notes, responses to reading, teaching plans—from my experiences as a writing center tutor in 1986 to the start of my student teaching in 1988 to my last year as an adjunct instructor in 1997. I focus on that period of time because it was when I seemingly had the least authority to assert curriculum, whether it was a matter of teaching within predetermined curricula or learning about new teaching assignments with barely a week to prepare. I was being disciplined by the "intended" curriculum of others, as well as by my station in life as a part-time adjunct writing instructor, one of those we called "freeway flyers" back in California. Curriculum was determined by others, and I was, on the whole, merely a delivery mechanism. Yet that time also offered glimpses of the ways writing classes and writing centers *could* be liberatory, could offer students opportunities for agency and authority over their lives via literacy. What I was learning were the possibilities for schooling as both a means of social control and a means of possibility. I don't think I spent a lot of time thinking about this contradiction when I was in a class or a writing center, but the intended curriculum and the means of assessment I was the face of in those settings often embodied that contradiction. It was as seemingly natural as the walls, desks, and blackboards, but no less constructed.

OF PARAGRAPHS AND GRAMMAR WORKBOOKS

My first experience with teaching was in the fall of 1986 as a writing center tutor while pursing my MA in creative writing at San Jose State. I ended up in the writing center because I was not hired for a TA position to teach a writing class. It was the latter that I really wanted, but, as someone with zero teaching experience at the time and only conceptual knowledge of what a writing class might do, based on my one semester of experience as a student in a class about teaching writing, I was woefully unqualified. Plus, never having taken first-year writing myself, but instead a first-year seminar on adolescent psychology at the University of Pennsylvania to which writing was somehow vaguely connected, I really had no clue.

The writing center at San Jose State was directed at the time by Scott Rice, who had great visibility outside of the English department for his work with the annual Bulwer-Lytton contest for really bad writing. But I had never come to the writing center as a student. After all, I was there to write fiction, had never heard of writing centers before that moment, and, as a writer with ambitions, surely did not imagine that *I* would need a writing tutor!

Still, I decided to apply to work in the writing center, and I remember that process involving a grammar/usage exam and a student writing sample to which we offered written feedback. The exam I essentially failed, having no real knowledge of formal grammar, but I must have done well enough on the response to the student sample to show an inkling of promise. The writing center agreed to hire me contingent on my taking a class in English grammar, one that was largely populated by teacher education students, for whom it was a requirement.

Somewhere around that time, the writing center also shifted in purpose from a drop-in center for all students to a center focused solely on working with students in basic writing or developmental English classes, who were required to attend the writing center one hour per week. During half of that time slot students worked on a "paragraph" they were required to compose for that particular meeting, and during the other half they worked through Teresa Glazier's *The Least You Should Know about English*, a grammar/usage workbook. Our job was to give feedback on the paragraph and to check on students' progress in the workbook (which had the answers to the exercises in the back; I suppose we were supposed to explain why those answers were correct).

I worked largely with students of color, many of whom were multilingual, who had been consigned to basic writing because of poor previous academic preparation or because most of their prior schooling had been in a language other than English. The work was dynamic and highly problematic. The paragraphs seem decontextualized and disconnected from whatever it was the students were writing in class, and a paragraph seemed an arbitrary container size for the thoughts and experiences they were trying to express. The grammar/usage worksheets were deadly dull and bore little relationship to students' paragraph writing; they could ace the worksheets but still have those errors show up in their paragraph writing.

By this time, it was becoming clear to me that a career as a writing teacher was a much more viable option than a career as a fiction writer, so, as I noted above, I then enrolled in a program to receive my high school English credential at the same time I was getting my MA. The curriculum of that program focused on liberatory pedagogy, and from our readings and writing, my classmates and I argued heatedly about schools as oppressive environments that strictly regulated students' literacies *and* about the possibilities for schools to be agents of liberation.

My work in the SJSU Writing Center with basic writing students who were being highly regulated seemed subversive on many levels, even if it was just that I was asking about and listening to my students' stories as readers and writers and human beings with complicated histories and lives, all of whom wanted nothing but opportunities for success. Writing center work, then, brought together my interests in teaching, learning, and social justice, and I became more aware of the complexities of these endeavors as well as of their vital importance.

I can see now that we were asserting conflicting curricula in those writing center sessions: the official curriculum signaled by required visits, one-paragraph limits, and remediation versus the curriculum we felt we might offer those basic writing students, an inkling of writing as a liberatory practice. Whether we had the power as graduate students to persuade students that our curriculum was superior to that created by the basic writing program and its teachers, I do not know. But it certainly gave me a clear view of the possibilities for writing centers as subversive sites of curriculum and pedagogy.

THE ROOKIE

I'm not sure why I raised my hand when the high school's vice principal asked who was willing to be a student teacher in an English-as-a-second language (ESL) classroom. I didn't have any specific ESL training up to that point. Sure, I had been working with non-native English speakers in the San Jose State Writing Center, but this would be different. This would be a ninth-grade class at Silver Creek High School in San Jose, a class full of fourteen-year-olds: teenagers, hormonal teenagers. And it would be my first student-teaching experience, a six-week testing ground that might tell me that the last thing I should do is try to teach anything to fourteen-year-olds, much less English to non-native teenagers. Or maybe my experience would be *To Sir with Love*, a triumph of the outsider teacher transforming a class of hardscrabble and kicked-to-the-curb teens, winning their trust, their affection, their love. And just like Sidney Poitier, I would be forced to leave at the end of my six weeks, the students standing on their chairs and clapping rhythmically, shouting, "Captain, my captain!" while LuLu breaks into song, the tears streaming down her face, cutting channels through her thick eyeliner (yes, in my mind the heroic-teacher film genre references all combine.).

At the time, however, I just wanted to survive. The expectations for my role were pretty straightforward. I would observe Mrs. Z's teaching for two weeks, have the class as my own for the next two, and then, depending on whether or not (or how many times) the local police were called in to intervene, I would either retreat to observer status for the final two weeks or continue to teach the class on my own.

Mrs. Z was a kindly woman. My memory of her was that she was quick to smile, probably in her mid-thirties (and, given that I was twenty-eight at the time, not much older than I), a nice, white, well-meaning person who took a rather maternal approach to her students. They were there to learn English, after all, so Mrs. Z started them at the beginning: with nursery rhymes. Something about these ninth-graders from Vietnam, Korea, Sudan, Mexico, or El Salvador reciting those nursery rhymes in their heavily accented English did not sit well with me. I'm not sure the students really minded or found it demeaning. One student from Vietnam whose name was Lam was teased a bit when they all recited "Mary Had a Little Lamb." But overall, they took on the challenge, the memorization and recitation of nursery rhymes, with little protest, if not some measure of enthusiasm.

In our teacher education class meetings previous to this experience, we discussed Freire's (1968) *Pedagogy of the Oppressed* and the history of American schooling to replicate status quo hierarches and prepare non-elite students for nonelite careers. We created mini lessons on "power" and "access" and "democracy" and wound ourselves tightly around the ways that we would all undo the great harm that had been perpetuated on the underclass, those very students I was now facing in my ninth-grade ESL class at Silver Creek High School. These sensibilities played a strong role in what I saw and did in that first student-teaching experience. From my observations while leading a reading group: "During reading I asked my group if they had thought of anything they wanted to learn in English that they weren't being taught in school. They still had no answer. I found that discouraging. But I'll keep asking." From my notes on preparing to teach on my own in that ESL class:

> Mon and Tue I have to teach out of the grammar book. It's a unit on using conjunctive adverbs: however, furthermore, nevertheless, etc. This includes a story about a guy named Finnegan who works for the railroad and has the problem of writing telegrams that are too long, therefore too expensive, about train wrecks. It ends with his shortest telegram, "On again, off again, gone again, Finnegan." The exercises are then about the connectors. There is no attempt to relate this to students' everyday lives. This is a class full of Asian immigrants. How absurd. I'm going to have them write about their weekends in brief, telegram form. We'll do my weekend as an example. Take that, Ira Shor.

Two weeks passed quickly, and it became my turn to teach. Mrs. Z charged me with teaching a unit on "transportation," which meant I would need to teach as much vocabulary as possible having to do with buses and cars and trains and boats and such. Mrs. Z gave me one more bit of direction, likely intended to curb my idealistic enthusiasm. "Don't have them write paragraphs," she told me. "They can't yet write paragraphs."

My goal for that unit, of course, became for students to write paragraphs. My approach was to use "transportation" as what Freire (1968) describes as a "generative theme," a significant idea from students' lives from which they could think and act critically upon the nature of their existences, cast off their shackles of oppression, and seize the power that was rightly theirs. I created flashcards with pictures of common forms of transportation on one side and the name of that transportation device on the other: bicycle, car, train, bus. And my first lesson was to have students identify the card that represented how they came to the United States, to write that story, to, yes, complete a full paragraph. They would then share those stories, give one other feedback, revise based on that response, and we'd create a collection of these stories, a kind of class publication, our record and reclamation of our literate lives.

Truthfully, I don't quite remember how that lesson went. I don't recall any great disasters or any great triumphs. My students approached their work with enthusiasm, but that was true when they were reciting "Mary Had a Little Lamb." I can say that they all did write paragraphs, complete stories of their journeys to the United States in whatever level of English they could master. And those levels became even more complicated in the six weeks I was in that class. I learned that if a ninth-grader who moved into the school district needed to be in an ESL class, that student would show up on Monday morning in mine, no matter his or her level of English proficiency. From week to week, the numbers of students grew, their proficiency levels grew more varied, and the brand-new student teacher from the university a few miles away did not have much of a clue.

I do not want to give the impression that I was in any way heroic in my first experience as a student teacher. One of my strongest memories is from one of my last days in that class, when another teacher would conduct a mandatory observation and then file a report that would be part of my application for a high school teaching credential. The evening before, when I had hoped to prepare, I needed to be at a social affair in San Francisco, some event related to my wife's world as a scientist. I recall that we stayed overnight in the city and the next morning I awoke very early to drive down to San Jose and meet my class. I figured I'd come up with a lesson on my way down. Maybe something that involved small-group work and lots of silent writing. Maybe something having to do with the Beatles songs I was asking them to memorize (perhaps just as much of a cultural imposition as nursery rhymes, but at least the themes were ones teenagers could relate to). It didn't go well. My students were far more disruptive than they had been at any other time. I really could not control the class. The observing teacher was not happy. I learned about the importance of preparation. And it would be a full year before my second student teaching experience, this one a semester long in a middle-class high school in Cupertino, one in which I would have sole charge of two classes and a supporting role in a third. None was an ESL class. There was no meeting with the vice principal and no opportunity to volunteer.

HANGING LOOSE AT HOMESTEAD

Homestead High School in Cupertino, California, was a staid, solid-looking brick and steel structure in a quiet suburban neighborhood in a middle-class county in the heart of Silicon Valley. When I did my stint as a student teacher there from January to June 1989, the parents of my students were likely middle managers at HP and Dell and Apple or owners of small businesses or more professional types, lawyers and doctors, poised to upscale their lifestyles with a move to Los Altos or Los Gatos or, for those with particularly high aspirations, Palo Alto or Menlo Park. Homestead High School was a contrast to my previous placement at Silver Creek High School, a school for new immigrants' kids or whoever might find themselves among the largely poor, largely Latino and Asian side of town.

My primary assignments at Homestead were to teach a junior-level writing class and an SAT prep elective (though the honors kids who populated that class seemed to approach it as required). The class of juniors was not particularly memorable other than my struggle to motivate these suburban kids to appreciate the finer points of English composition. I was following a set curriculum, nothing particularly inspiring, though I do remember that my approach to writing an evaluative argument was to ask students to bring in their favorite songs and make an argument as to why the rest of the class should like them, too. They dutifully did what I asked, with minimal enthusiasm, walking through their required classes as good student workers do, largely without passion, fulfilling a demand made on them by a system over which they had little control. It was good preparation for the rest of their lives.

The grammar prep course was a bit more combative, at least when it came to student reaction to my collaborative, student-centered teaching methods. I particularly remember one student's reflection at the end of the year: "School is not a democracy; you should lecture more." In my mind, that student was one of my best, cheerfully identifying parts of speech, building her vocabulary, and correcting grammar errors in our workbook. I had no sense of the resentment she was building over my approach to teaching.

I also spent a short time in a creative writing class, just enough to teach a lesson I created on writing about dreams, using Joseph Campbell and Carl Jung to justify my approach. When I debriefed on that lesson with the classroom teacher, he commended me on my enthusiasm and somewhat wistfully remembered back to when he felt a similar passion for teaching.

In my journal I wrote: "One of the hardest things about this high school teaching is dealing with the overwhelming negativity. The kids don't want to be here. They're used to being bored, worksheeted to death. It's one thing to motivate them to do the work; it's another to make them enjoy it. Many teachers become negative in the face of this student reaction and an insensitive and unpredictable bureaucracy." And a few pages later, this: "Make knowledge relevant and problematic and have transformative potential. You can't have self-empowerment without social empowerment." In the journal I kept from that period, I wrote about having coffee with my friend Bob, who was an engineering graduate student, catching up on each other's lives. I wrote, "I like teaching writing. Bob says I sound like the classic wide-eyed, change-the-world neophyte (he didn't mean it in a derogatory sense). I replied that I couldn't go into it any other way."

I certainly do not want to portray myself as a heroic educator, bringing my brand of enlightened, liberatory curriculum to those who really needed it. My journals and teaching notebooks of the time certainly demonstrate my ability to pre-judge my students, to put the responsibility squarely on their shoulders—and thus not on mine. From my notes on teaching a junior-level high school writing class in my second student teaching experience:

> The only student who is still resisting me is Jason Neff, who hates writing and is shallow and immature. He also has a lot of fear in his life, of failure, of authority, but I can't tell him that writing will help him with this. He recognizes the system as one that gives little help and plays nicely into that system. He corrupts it with passive-aggressive behavior, eeks out his C, and will grow up to transfer his oppression onto co-workers, children, or spouse. Perhaps I'm being too harsh (oh, probably), but I think Neff is typical of most students around here. They are resistant to any real learning because it requires much more than a system that only asks that they

be obedient, fill out worksheets, and arrive to class on time. Fulfilling the latter will allow you to pass any high school curriculum.

Fulfilling the former allows you to grab control over your own life. Will Neff ever learn this? I don't think he will from my class.

The moment when I saw the faculty in their most joyful state was the last day of the year, when they were poised for summer vacation, when the school was largely free of students, when they could pack up their classrooms and put the year's lessons and successes and failures behind them. For me, a student teacher poised at the start of a career in the classroom, it was not exactly a ringing endorsement.

FROM SERVICE MANAGER TO TEACHER

My college-teaching career began with a telephone call. I was working as a service manager in a bicycle shop in Palo Alto, a position I had held for only two weeks in the late summer of 1989 when that phone rang. It was the math coordinator at a local community college. He had gotten my name from someone at my MA program at San Jose State. Would I come teach first-year writing at his college?

I said what immediately came to mind—I had just taken this job (my first-ever salaried job with benefits), I was only two weeks in, there was no way I could quit and come teach for him. I thanked him for the offer and hung up. About thirty seconds later, he called back, telling me that they were trying to fill a Saturday class, which might not interfere with my bike shop schedule. Could I pick that one up? Well, in the thirty seconds between calls, I had engaged in a mental reckoning. There I was, recent holder of both an MA in English and a high school teaching credential, working as a service manager in a bicycle shop. Now, I don't mean any disrespect to bike shop service managers, but my degrees were not exactly being put to use. And my student teaching experience, concluded just a few months prior, gave me some idea that I could be a pretty good writing teacher, that students responded to the opportunities I tried to create for them, that I wanted to be part of a community of learners and teachers. And I felt like I was a pretty mediocre service manager (only two weeks in, impatient customers, unmotivated employees, and a clueless boss were driving me crazy!). When the math coordinator called back, I asked to be able to think about his offer that night and let him know for sure the next day.

That evening, my wife and I went out to our favorite Japanese restaurant and made a list of pros and cons for teaching writing versus bike shop career on a paper placemat. In the end, teaching writing won out, and the next day I agreed to teach two classes at the community college and then a third at San Jose State and gave two weeks' notice at the bike shop. For that last week, I was doing both jobs as the fall semester started at the community college, an unfortunately common situation as an adjunct, getting hired with barely a week to prepare (much less being hired by the math coordinator to teach writing classes).

I loved my community college students. On the whole, they were older adults, returning to school to better their lives. They were racially and ethnically diverse, reflecting the community of the San Jose area. They readily engaged in the activities I asked them to do—exploring personal experience, playing with language, collaborating with one other in group work and peer review—with enthusiasm, wit, and determination. While the previous semester I had figured that my future would be as a high school English teacher, that community college experience offered a view of higher education as fulfilling the goals I had as a teacher, a place where my curriculum might thrive rather than meet resistance. Emboldened by these experiences, in my journal at the time, I wrote the following: "Connecting to a student's life and the life of her family to her education is central to success in learning. Too often the model of teaching that is so common is disconnected from a student's life. It's as if school is the time to leave everything behind, to be a blank slate, to be a sponge, to absorb. Instead we must rely on the cultural heritage of all of our students to create the curriculum of the class."

That October 1989, a major earthquake hit the San Francisco Bay Area, delaying the World Series and causing injury, destruction, and disruption for everyone. In my community college classes, about half my students never showed up once school reopened. The stability in many of their lives, tentative before the earthquake, was now disrupted. My curriculum was overwhelmed by circumstance.

WRITE UNTIL IT GLOWS

One of my more unusual teaching gigs was teaching writing onsite to nuclear power plant employees. My students were enrolled in a University of Maryland University College BS degree program, a requirement put into place by the Nuclear Regulatory Commission after the Three-Mile Island nuclear accident in 1979. I would either drive or fly to a range of sites—from South Carolina to New Jersey to Pennsylvania to Wisconsin. While there, I would run three or four multi-hour workshops, often for employees coming off of twelve-hour work shifts. I truly learned the value of active learning, of keeping students active, sharing, doing, as just a few minutes of my droning on would result in nodding heads and heavy eyelids.

On the whole, my students were my age or older, largely navy veterans, as serving on nuclear subs qualified them to work in the nuclear industry. For the most part they lived in rural areas—where these plants were sited—and held fairly conservative beliefs when it came to social and governmental policy. Yet many were also strongly anti-authoritarian, eager to learn workplace communication so that they would have an advantage over their bosses, whom they saw as poor leaders and poor communicators. It was thrilling to spend a visit teaching techniques for writing persuasive memos and then come back in six weeks to hear my students' stories of composing those memos for specific workplace purposes and being rewarded for their strong writing.

The curriculum itself was well established for all of us, from the choice of textbooks to the specific graded assignments to the grading scale. UMUC dealt with quality control by regularizing the curriculum. Not exactly teacher-proof materials, but at least teacher-resistant in a way. Of course, that left it up to me how to engage students with those materials, and teaching in workplace settings created powerful exigency to put the various assignments into practice. I could still assert my values of writing as agentive, but I was also learning about genres far afield from the personal writing and personal exploration that had been central to my curriculum up to that point, particularly with developmental writing classes for community college students. Workplace writing was, indeed, "genre as social action" as Carolyn Miller (1984) describes, with high stakes for students, as they both were affected by what others wrote and could bring about intended effect by what they wrote.

In one of my last nuclear power plant gigs, students were at a government-controlled site, one that produced weapons in addition to hosting a nuclear power plant (and I needed to obtain a low-level security clearance in order to gain entrance—I was told to avoid the poppy seed bagels that morning.). Rumors were abundant that the site would be closed, part of an overall contraction across government sites. My students seemed even more eager than previously to master the communication skills they felt they needed to be successful in their jobs. Many were transitioning to work in the area of environmental cleanup, bringing to bear their knowledge of the nuclear industry and its hazards, along with their writing skills, to a strong societal need. Their own pragmatic curricula well complemented the established goals of the course and my own desires to shape their learning experiences. This curricular intersection has not been a given, in my experience, particularly when it comes to required writing courses. But it certainly should be our goal.

SORRY, TRY AGAIN

One of the oddest incidences in my time as a part-time writing instructor came near the end of this period, when I applied to teach in a large writing program in the Boston area (best left unnamed) while I finished my dissertation. A fellow tutor at the MIT Writing Center, where I was tutoring sixteen hours per week, had been teaching for that program and encouraged me to apply. I remember a somewhat awkward interview with the writing program director, who was not a compositionist but instead a literary scholar who had dabbled a bit in the scholarship of teaching writing (he had a *College English* article to his credit, which I dutifully toted along and made reference to during my interview with him). Whatever my sense of awkwardness, the WPA called me soon after to offer me a section of first-year writing, though I would first have to submit a writing sample to be scrutinized by an unnamed hiring committee. As a doctoral student in education, I did not think my seminar papers would be appropriate for such a sample, but fortunately I had just had my first scholarly article accepted for publication in *Composition Studies* (Lerner 1996), so that's what I submitted in an effort to dot and cross the appropriate letters. A few days later, the WPA called to tell me that there was a problem with my writing sample. Could I submit another?

What was the problem? I asked. He couldn't tell me, he responded, but could I submit another? How could I submit another without knowing the problem with the first? I asked. The WPA did not have an answer, saying the matter was largely out of his hands, but that they couldn't hire me without an acceptable writing sample. I told him I would look for something else to submit.

A day or so later, I wrote a brief email to the WPA, telling him that I wouldn't be submitting another sample, that the situation was absurd, and that I would be finding teaching work somewhere else. He responded quickly, telling me that he'd talk to the committee, go out on a limb for me, and that I could expect to teach that section the upcoming term. Which I did.

I never learned what the problem was with my writing sample. It perhaps was a result of the content: that article was a historical analysis of required first-year writing courses, particularly the ways that English departments had exploited first-year writing instructors and students for various ends, whether to keep graduate programs robust, to ensure full-time equivalent revenue, or to enforce status quo literacy standards. Yeah, in retrospect that might not have been the best sample to send to get hired to teach first-year writing in a traditional English department, but I figured those nameless, faceless readers would be open minded, that their version of the curriculum for first-year writing would either be aligned with mine or that they'd simply appreciate the historical critique. That was not a correct calculation.

TEACHERS TEACHING TEACHERS

Some of the most influential experiences in my development as a teacher involved taking part in local National Writing Project courses—offered by the San Jose–Area Writing Project in 1989 and 1990—and two NWP Summer Institutes—in San Jose in 1991 and Northern Virginia in 1992. While these experiences could be described as largely pedagogical—developing specific classroom strategies to engage students from kindergarten to college as writers—my NWP experiences were also curricular in the ways I needed to express my values as a writing teacher, both in terms of what I wanted my students to learn and how I saw that learning best enabled.

The culminating task in both Summer Institutes was to offer a complete writing lesson, both engaging our fellow teachers in the lesson itself and describing the rationale, implementation, and variations on that activity. At my first Summer Institute in San Jose, my lesson was to have students explore the worst job they had ever held. My purpose was to have students perform a variety of invention activities—listing jobs held, generating questions to interview a classmate on his/her worst job, writing an account of that job experience, and then to move from the specific to the abstract, working with others to make generalizations or abstractions based on each other's worst job experiences. This was a version of what Ira Shor describes in *Critical Teaching and Everyday Life* (1987), drawing from Freire's concept of the "generative theme." And it was an activity I used each semester in my community college writing courses, where my students had long histories as workers and where choosing the worst experience was unfortunately difficult because there were so many to choose from. My attempt to build students' critical consciousness about their labor histories was a clear assertion of curriculum co-constructed with students, whether knowledge assertions about the labor itself or about the ways certain kinds of labor are more valued than others in our society.

This activity represented to me the ideal of how I wanted to perform in the classroom: creating the conditions for students to think and write critically about their lives, to gain agency through writing and reflection, to share their work in a community of writers. At that Summer Institute, I also extended that activity on work to encompass four themes that I felt were central to all of my students' lives: work, family/self, school, community. I would ask students to read and write based on these themes, conduct on-the-ground research in each of these sites and, essentially, follow a curriculum that I felt was relevant and powerful.

Over the next several years in my life as an adjunct instructor, it was only in a few classes that I was able to fully explore this thematic approach. Instead, the "intended" curriculum as expressed by required textbooks and predetermined syllabi and assignments were more often what I taught. And once I began teaching courses other than basic writing and first-year writing, particularly business communication, literature, and film study, the content and curriculum of those specific areas dominated. It also occurred to me that while I intended my curriculum to speak broadly to students' experiences and interests, I really was not engaging with them to develop topics for reading and writing—my students and I were not co-constructing curriculum. My class was not a version of Ira Shor's *When Students Have Power* (1996), in which Shor ceded nearly all curricular and evaluative decisions to his community college students. I want to think that this reluctance was largely a result of my status at the time—part-time instructor plying his trade at multiple institutions, usually having been hired with little time to prepare. But fully trusting my students, fully engaging with them to co-create curriculum, is difficult stuff. It might not work for all. Some students might tell me, "School is not a democracy; you need to lecture more." And I'm not yet sure how I should respond.

FULL-TIME CURRICULUM

For the last twenty years, I have been very fortunate to have been employed full-time as a writing instructor, though over that time my roles have varied as I went from faculty in a non-tenure-granting institution to a non-tenure-stream full-time lecturer to my current role at Northeastern as a tenured faculty member in the English department, where I've held administrative positions as writing center director (twice!), director of writing in the disciplines, and writing program director. In my first full-time teaching position, I was situated in a college of pharmacy and health sciences teaching a two-semester first-year writing sequence and a detective fiction and film elective as well as coordinating the writing center and the writing program. That did not mean that my curriculum necessarily stabilized or that I was able to co-create curriculum with my students in the ways I call for in this book. Teaching writing, in whatever context, is always contested, always a struggle between an instructor's goals and values, the goals and values of the institution, and the goals, values, and experiences students bring to classrooms and writing centers. My point is that struggle largely exists under the surface, mostly hidden from view or overwhelmed by the "intended" and "taught" curricula.

Until I came to Northeastern, my full-time teaching career largely involved teaching students in STEM fields, whether at Massachusetts College of Pharmacy & Health Sciences or later at MIT. At MIT in particular, my teaching was akin to being a writing fellow: I was a "writing specialist" attached to communications-intensive laboratory courses in science or engineering. My students were writing about their empirical research created in the lab, and the focus was on the genres of scientific articles, posters, and presentations. In many ways, I felt a long way from my beginnings in liberatory pedagogy, but then again, the writing, speaking, and visualizing tasks that students were doing were authentic, often based on novel research rather than pre-planned results, and relevant to their present and future writing lives. Still, the writing curriculum in these circumstances was largely about writing as a tool, a very powerful tool, but not one that necessarily could vie for disciplinary status. Writing was subservient to disciplinary knowledge making, seemingly neutral when it came to questions of power and prestige, of whose ideas should count most, and how expression of those ideas is highly regulated. In the formulation of writing in the disciplines, or WID, the D carries far more power than the W.

As a tenured faculty member, my access to and authority over curriculum are far more present than during my time as an adjunct instructor, and the last several years that I have spent as a member of my university's Faculty Senate have reinforced the importance of faculty "ownership" and oversight of curriculum. This importance makes it even more crucial, in my view, for writing studies faculty—full-time and part-time—to exercise that authority, but in ways consistent with our values and beliefs in student agency and the power of literacy. Still, the curricula that we might bring to bear in our classrooms or writing centers has limits, particularly for students who take curriculum into their own hands, as I describe in the next chapter.

4
TEACHING AND TUTORING TERRORISTS

The two stories I tell in this chapter are unlike others in this book in that they are not classroom or writing center accounts of teachers and students delivering, receiving, or negotiating curriculum. Instead, the students I describe follow a long tradition of the extracurriculum (Applebee 1974; Gere 1994), or what it might mean when students create their own writing curricula outside of the classroom. Writing teachers, after all, have long been committed to writing as a lifelong practice, as a means to gain agency and participate in civic and community life (Bazerman et al. 2017; Roozen 2010) or, simply, as a way to record and make sense of one's experiences (Numrich 1996). What happens in the classroom ideally prepares students for these out-of-school and post-graduation experiences with writing. But this relationship cannot be assumed. Students' writing lives often exist and flourish outside of—or, more accurately, parallel to—what they're doing in our classrooms, a tradition that dates at least to the nineteenth century (Applebee 1974, 12; Rudolph 1990, ch. 7). Whether they have full literate lives as bloggers or new-media mixers (Davis and Yancey 2014; Yancey 2004) or participate in online communities devoted to fan fiction (Black 2009) or gaming (Gee 2007) or explore writing in ways that are not cultivated in classrooms (e.g., Kinloch, Burkhard, and Penn 2017), students are creating curricula for and by themselves, untethered from frameworks for success, outcome statements, or high-stakes testing.

It's a bit too easy to romanticize these agentive actions, to point out the failings of school and to applaud students for taking control of their learning. Certainly, some applause is called for here, but writing is never neutral, never existing without consequences. For the two students I write about in this chapter, the consequences are lengthy federal prison sentences. Writing served and failed both though in very different ways. An essential point to this chapter, as well as to this entire book, is that curriculum is an expression of values, whether to critique current notions of normativity or to reinforce that status quo. That's the

DOI: 10.7330/9781607328810.c004

essential mechanism for—and barrier to—reform and why I am arguing in this book for attention to curriculum: the opportunities we create for students to write in meaningful ways are dependent on a curriculum, not merely pedagogy. In most of schooling, particularly in K–12 public school settings, curriculum is an attempt to replicate "mainstream" values (Anyon 1980; Heath 1984), and for students outside of that mainstream, those whose race, class, gender, abilities, and/or sexuality has marked them for a sidestream, one that's running dry, their disengagement with curriculum is a cultural disengagement. The movement for "culturally responsive classrooms" (e.g., Gay 2000) or "culturally relevant education" (Aronson and Laughter 2016) is an attempt to address this disengagement, but much of that literature is focused on pre-college schooling. The two students I write about in this chapter created their own curricula largely after their undergraduate years.

Violations of normalcy or of the status quo also have limits. While critique of the mainstream has a key function to question long-held beliefs and work toward social justice, some norms are in the service of social stability and harmony. In other words, not all norms are meant to be violated, particularly those in place to ensure the safety of others. Still, what is a clear violation in some instances is much murkier in others, and in those latter cases norms might be used as a cudgel, as an expression of state power in which the power itself, often delivered through writing, is the lasting legacy. The stories I tell in this chapter occupy both of those possibilities: state power expressed through enforcement of law, clear cut in one case and far more disturbing in the other.

That my teaching career intersected with both students whose stories I tell in this chapter might be merely coincidence or a remarkable twist of fate. I wonder, however, about the writing lives of many of our students outside and beyond school, writing lives we rarely hear about or track. I wonder what would happen if we planned more carefully for those inevitable writing lives, specifically when it comes to curriculum, if we worked with students to ensure "expansive framing" (Engle et al. 2012) for the kinds of writing they might do not just in our classes and in our writing centers, but outside of school-sanctioned contexts. I won't claim with certainty that we would alter the outcome that befell the two students I describe in this chapter, but I also can't help but wonder if it would have.

TUTORING THE CASE WESTERN SHOOTER

For writing centers, a common curricular feature is resistance to "normal" teaching practices found in the writing classroom, captured in a

1951 CCCC workshop account noting that "the writing laboratory should be what the classroom often is not—natural, realistic, and friendly" ("Organization and Use of a Writing Laboratory" 18). In writing center literature since then, the assertion of writing centers as resistant to our institutions' mainstream language practices is commonplace. Kevin Davis (1995), for example, urges an embrace of the "fringe": "Any program which seeks to regularize the writing center's function is diametrically opposed to the very founding principles of the center. Our heritage, our lives place us on the fringe of the academy and to leave that fringe is to abandon who we are and what we do" (6). Along similar lines, Terrance Riley (1994) warns against writing centers becoming mainstream, noting that "our most exhilarating successes derive from our intermediate, outside-the-mainstream status vis-à-vis the university" (28).

In the day-to-day lives of writing centers, this notion of "alternative space" is usually found in descriptions of the writing center as a kind of "oasis" in the midst of the barren landscape of our institutions. Examples include the University of California, San Diego, where OASIS stands for the Office of Instructional Support and Academic Services, including tutoring in writing (https://students.ucsd.edu/sponsor/oasis/). Additional oases can be found at Rhode Island College (https://www .ric.edu/oasis/), Iowa Wesleyan University (https://www.iw.edu/writing -support/), Husson University (http://www.husson.edu/academics/aca demic-support-oasis/writing-center/), Western Illinois College, where the writing center describes itself as "in the heart of campus, an oasis for writers" (http://www.wiu.edu/cas/english/university_writing_center /newsletter/WritingMatters.pdf), and the Hawk Writing Center of Hayfield Secondary School, which offers on its blog that "the writing center should be an oasis in the desert of stress occupied by the rest of the school" (http://hawkwritingcenter.weebly.com/blog).

While the oasis analogy does have a certain romantic appeal, several scholars have pointed out that it is a construction that contains its own set of exclusions. For example, Nancy Grimm (1996) tells us that "writing centers are often inadvertently implicated in the regulatory uses of literacy" (6) and that they "operate with structures of privilege (i.e., historically racist institutions) and often the principles and practices we most take for granted support these structures of privilege, thereby placing responsibility for change on the shoulders of the individuals who use writing centers, individuals who are often in the least powerful social position" (Grimm 2011, 79). Jackie Grutsch McKinney (2005) critiques the "comfort" metaphor many writing centers use to mark their spaces/oases, pointing out how such constructs are potentially exclusionary when they come from a particular socioeconomic ideal: "We might recreate the familiar patterns of our class or culture's idea of home: guests are greeted at the front door, led to a sitting room or table for dining, escorted back to the front door after the visit, and asked to return. These patterns might not be shared by all students, particularly in writing centers, when our clientele might include a greater proportion of students who are not white or privileged or American than the general university population" (16). These scholars show that the writing center's assertion of curriculum as resistance to certain norms (e.g., classrooms as restrictive spaces) contains its own set of normative values ("comfort" and "home") or its own value-laden curriculum that not all students might embrace.[1]

Student resistance, however, is not ignored in writing center literature and practice. Working with resistant or hostile student writers is the stuff of many tutor-training manuals and tutor-meeting conversations. The roles that tutors and students perform in a session—whether "minimalist" (Brooks 1991) or "directive" (Shamoon and Burns 1995) on the tutors' part—speak to a certain interactive ideal or knowledge assertions (i.e., curriculum) about tutor and writer roles. When this ideal is resisted, its assumptions, limits, and—potentially—harm might be revealed. When resistant writers ask for our feedback but then belittle our strategic advice, we want to flip the appointment book page, move on, save our good stuff for writers who might be more appreciative. We've reached our limits, our norms violated, our curricular values challenged. For the student I focus on next, resistance was the operating norm, and the story of Biswanath Halder speaks to the limits of resisting and violating norms, whether in the writing center or in the culture at large.

In the spring of 1995, I was in my penultimate year in a doctorate in education program at Boston University, and I was tutoring in one of the university's writing centers. My dissertation was a participant-observation study of that center, an attempt to understand the language that tutors and students used to assert their roles and responsibilities in sessions. Several of my fellow graduate student tutors were recording their sessions for me that semester or, if not recording, bringing my attention to particular noteworthy sessions, for whatever reason.

Biswanath Halder showed up in the writing center in the third week in March with an application essay to an MBA program in hand and proceeded over the next two weeks and the course of eleven tutoring sessions to challenge not just our notions of effective writing center practice and appropriate student behavior, but our tolerance, our middle-class privilege, our acceptance of difference. In sum, he challenged *our* curricular notions of the writing center as an oasis or a safe space. And Halder would come to challenge many others' notions of academic environments—whether writing centers or the whole institution—as safe havens.

From the get-go, Halder shopped around with the tutoring staff, meeting with six of the eight of us, seemingly looking for some quality that would appeal to his sense of what our roles as tutors should be. Here's the comment Sylvia wrote on her evaluation sheet after being the first tutor to conference with him: "Difficult meeting because this student seemed almost hostile or aggressive and expected an immediate, definitive 'answer,' rather than a suggestion of how to edit a paragraph or choose the proper word. Maybe it's just some cultural dissonance here? Ask me about him, Neal. <u>Strange</u> . . ."[2]

For Sylvia and for the rest of us, the strangeness of Halder was in part physical: his age relative to ours (he was much older), his status as an international student from India, his foul breath, his ill-fitting toupee, his complicated system of multicolored highlighting illuminating his words. Most of all, though, it was his hostile attitude, his way of resisting most of what we said but repeatedly returning for another session. While it's painful to admit now, Halder became the fodder for a great deal of our conversation and joking; we simply made fun of him at our staff meetings and social occasions. He was a stock comic character in our serious academic lives. We even had a nickname for him—Bimmy. We knew of course, that ridiculing Bimmy was just plain wrong, but the social glue of that adolescent humor won the day. We could have a beer, make fun of Bimmy, and assert our place and authority in a world in which graduate students—and writing center tutors—have little of each. I don't mean to excuse our behavior, however. We were exerting privilege, eschewing difference, enacting a hidden curriculum, castigating Halder with very little knowledge of his circumstances or of his motivations. We were asserting our comfortable place in the institution, where characters like Halder were only the odd occasional visitor.

Somehow, Halder and I reached a compromise of sorts, and I ended up working with him three or four times over those two weeks. At each conference, he would challenge my notions of nondirectiveness. When he'd ask for my views on the relative merits of two versions of a single sentence or paragraph, I quickly learned to forget about the stock writing center–approved, non direct response of "Well, what do you think?" and go right to choosing my favorite and indicating in as much depth as I could why I had made that choice. Immediately, Halder would disagree with me, and we'd move on to the next highlighted passage. Still, by the next time we met, I'd see that some of my suggested changes had worked their way into his text. He was accepting my expertise in his own resistant way; he believed in the power of words. Besides his MBA application, Halder was also working on a website intended as an information portal for Indian students worldwide, the "All-Indian Network," combining the power of technology and the power of language to bring about what he saw as necessary change.

While I've gone on to an academic career in writing studies, Biswanath Halder's future was far less positive.

On May 9, 2003, at 4 p.m., Halder, wearing a bulletproof vest and a military helmet and carrying two guns, "smashed his way through a locked rear door" (Kesegich 2003, 4) of the Frank Gehry–designed Peter B. Lewis Building on the Case Western Reserve University campus. He immediately shot and killed Norman Wallace, a first-year MBA student who had recently been elected president of the Black MBA Student Association and who, tragically, was in the wrong place at the wrong time. For the next seven hours, Halder held the faculty, students, and staff hostage in a building one account described as having "no right angles and hallways that dip and swerve" ("Cleveland Shooter" 2003).

By 11 p.m., a SWAT team managed to enter through the roof, subdue Halder with a shot to his shoulder, and capture him. Once arrested, Halder was charged with a 338-count indictment and, initially, a potential death penalty as a result of violating post 9/11 anti-terrorism statutes. In the end, after two years of trials and motions and psychiatrist reports and delays, Halder was found guilty of his crimes and sentenced to life in prison.

According to published reports, Biswanath Halder's actions were precipitated by a more than three-year legal struggle against Case Western employee Shawn Miller, who, Halder claimed, had hacked into and wiped out Halder's website (Hiaasen 2002). For Halder, that website, his carefully written manifesto for an "All-Indian Network" that he had revealed to us when we were his writing center tutors, represented "everything I had" in his quest "to solve mankind's problems through the Internet," according to his civil suit deposition. After losing his website, Halder engaged in more discursive activity: a flurry of letter writing and judicial action, all of which yielded no satisfaction. According to one account, "Court records, interviews and Halder's writings show that the bachelor led a life of awkward isolation while creating an Internet persona of a budding millionaire and social activist, even a savior of the world. There were plenty of contradictions" (Hiaasen and Mangels 2003).

The final violent act of this person described by neighbors in Cleveland's Little Italy neighborhood as "a classic loner who rarely spoke and walked down the middle of [the road] pulling a grocery cart filled with books" ("Cleveland Shooter" 2003) yielded little justice as well.

He had become a stereotype, the norm-violating loner-turned-violent killer, the "Case Western shooter," and pages and pages of news articles about him and his final act did little to delve deeply into the person who had been driven to such rage. Here's the lead to the *Cleveland Plain Dealer* story from April 2005: "Evidence abounds that Biswanath Halder is a bizarre and troubled man. But there isn't enough evidence that the 64-year-old loner from India is mentally incompetent to stand trial for the deadly 2003 shooting spree at Case Western Reserve University, a judge ruled Tuesday" (Nichols 2005). Halder became a stock character playing a stock role, just as he had been for my fellow graduate students and me.

Biswanath Halder's role as a stock character also took on a life in the Internet world. Immediately following the shooting, he became the subject of blogs and discussion boards across the political spectrum. For left-leaning Internet sites, his case was an example of the need for stricter gun-control laws. For right-leaning sites, Halder, who had publicly opposed U.S. involvement in Iraq, was an example of a peacenik's true colors and of terrorism right here at home. The information age's faith in the power of language has subsumed Halder himself, and his difference, his strangeness, had become the defining characteristic in world that eschews nuance and seeks definition in nicknames and stereotypes. His perceived violations of norms extended far and wide.

Biswanath Halder's personal writing curriculum, whether his application to the Case Western MBA program, his pan-Indian website, or his written attempts to receive justice for how he felt he had been wronged, largely existed outside of the official curriculum of schooling.

Words meant everything to Halder, and his struggles with me and my fellow tutors over specific wording defy notions of standard writing center curricula, which eschew a focus on language-level or "lower-order" concerns. Halder's incessant letter writing, court documents, and Internet postings all were words of higher-order concern meant to bring about what he saw as needed change in the world. Sadly, of course, the erasure of those words drove him to seek revenge, not with words, but with an assault weapon.

Ultimately, Biswanath Halder took an innocent person's life, wounded two others in his shooting rampage, and created psychological harm for many. He violated norms of civil society, no matter his motivation. His final act of resistance had consequences that would do little to reshape the norms he objected to. The senselessness of his rage is also testament to its ultimate futility. Many words have now been written about Halder, but few are about his notions of social justice and world peace. According to one account, "[Halder] believed he possessed the secrets to peace and prosperity for all mankind and graciously shared these nuggets of wisdom via his Web site—until someone deleted its entire contents from his computer" (Greene 2003).

Halder's extracurriculum is one of many instances of students and citizens placing an abiding faith in the power of writing to make changes in the world, but finding that those changes are difficult and perhaps dangerous to enact—and, in Halder's case, dangerous and fatal to others. Perhaps Halder's interactions with us back at Boston University should have been a red flag; his violation of our curricular values wasn't merely an occasion for our derision but a signal for action, for one of us—for me—to alert campus authorities. However, the ways in which we might be uncomfortable in tutoring sessions, whether due to student resistance or student difference, usually speak more to the hidden curriculum of a writing center and its implied values than to any specific action on students' parts. Of course and unfortunately, we have examples of students exhibiting dangerous behavior in writing center sessions and the ways tutoring staff might deal with such violation of norms (e.g., Hobson 1997). But Halder's case still makes me wonder how writing centers might encounter difference in ways that enable student agency.

Could such actions have made a difference in Biswanath Halder's fate? There's no way to answer that question, but there will be future Halders, and any effort to avert future tragedy is surely worthwhile.

Biswanath Halder's violation of societal norms was a clear case with little nuance. The next student I write about also had an abiding faith in the power of language to bring about meaningful change and to personalize the writing curriculum outside of school-sponsored venues. The consequences of his actions speak to the power of the state to assert particular norms or curricular values, even at the cost of violating the liberty of its citizens.

I TAUGHT A JIHADIST TO WRITE

Not long after my tutoring experiences with Biswanath Halder and after I'd completed my doctorate in education in 1996, I was hired into my first academic position at the Massachusetts College of Pharmacy & Health Sciences (MCPHS) in Boston. I applied for this job after seeing a help-wanted ad in the *Boston Globe*.

> Writing Center Coordinator (Half Time): The Division of Arts & Sciences
> at the Mass. College of Pharmacy is seeking an indiv. to assist composition
> faculty in diagnosis/remediation of writing problems among ESL and
> native writers of English; recruit, train & supervise peer tutors; provide
> direct tutoring services. M.A. in writing/rhetoric, specialized training in
> ESL & exp. using writing process approach with ESL and native writers of
> English and the ability to work with a diverse student body needed. This
> is a 20 hr/ wk, 9 month appointment offering a competitive salary. Start
> 8/27 with renewal contingent upon funding.

After a year of half-time employment at MCPHS, I was promoted to a
full-time assistant professor position with administrative responsibilities
for the writing center and first-year writing courses (see Lerner 2000
for more on this experience). At MCPHS, required writing was a two-
semester sequence with a cohort of students largely working with the
same instructor over both semesters. In the 2000–2001 academic year,
one of my students in that two-semester sequence was Tarek Mehanna.

Roughly nine years later, on October 21, 2009, Mehanna was arrested
on charges of "conspiring to provide material support to terrorists"
(March 2012). Mehanna, who, as you might guess, is a Muslim, was
then confined to the Plymouth County, Massachusetts, Correctional
Facility, where he awaited a jury trial. After six weeks of testimony, on
December 20, 2011, over two years after his initial arrest, Mehanna was
convicted and sentenced to seventeen and a half years in federal prison
(Akbar 2013). In November 2013, Mehann's appeal was turned down by
the U.S. Court of Appeals for the first circuit, and in October 2014 the
U.S. Supreme Court refused to rule on that appeal decision, effectively
affirming Mehanna's federal prison stint until 2028 (Andersen 2014).

Here are the questions I wonder about now: did the two semesters
Tarek Mehanna spend with me in required first-year composition and
the one semester in an elective humanities class play a role in where
he now finds himself? Did these writing and writing-intensive classes
contribute to the personalized writing curriculum of someone who was
convicted of fomenting terrorism through his writing and whose long
letters and poems from prison were distributed at his website? Or were
Mehanna's writing classes simply one of many requirements to fulfill in
his eventually receiving a doctorate in pharmacy, no more influential
than his required calculus or chemistry classes?

When Mehanna was my student, he earned a solid B, and I remember
him best not for what he wrote but for the fact that his father was one
of my faculty colleagues and that Mehanna bore a striking resemblance
to his Egyptian-born dad. For his first essay his freshman year, I asked
Mehanna and his classmates to define "caring," a topic that seemed

appropriate in a context in which every student was an aspiring health professional. In his essay, titled "Why Doesn't Society Care?" Mehanna took issue with what he saw as selfishness prevalent around him, writing, "Selfishness is a part of everyone's psyche, and it is the level of this selfishness which is present more in some than others that reflects the amount of caring in society." Mehanna in very general terms asserted that the "lack of caring" was epidemic in what he saw around him, whereas instead "caring should be more widely expressed between members of society." To this draft, I offered a B+, writing, "Tarek, Good job overall—my only quibble is with the need for more specific feedback/concrete evidence to support your contentions—that's what strong arguments need."

I look for more clues into Mehanna's future from what he produced for me over three courses, but ultimately, I don't find much. Instead, I try to piece together Mehanna's path from my writing classes to his present predicament, combing through newspaper accounts, blog postings, and federal indictments. According to the "Search and Seizure Warrant" issued for Mehanna's arrest, Mehanna's Dell laptop computer needed to be seized because "its contents constitute evidence of the commission of a criminal offense, contraband, fruits of crime, and things otherwise criminally possessed" (United States District Court 2). The Joint Terrorism Task Force was led to Mehanna's computer on the basis of testimony from two unnamed cooperating witnesses and from Daniel Maldonado, who at the time was serving a ten-year prison sentence for "receiving military-type training" from al-Qa'ida.

According to the *Boston Globe*, Mehanna was accused of "using a laptop as a weapon to try to radicalize others and incite jihad, or holy war" (Murphy 2010, A1). The gist of that charge is that Mehanna translated al-Qa'ida missives from Arabic to English and posted them on his blog. Words, language, writing: the elements of the charges on which Mehanna was convicted.

This interest in Mehanna's writing and computer was not new. Mehanna's arrest in 2009 was a follow-up to an incident in August 2006, when the Foreign Intelligence Surveillance Court authorized that this same computer's contents be examined, as well as a Joint Terrorism Task Force interview in December 2006 during which Mehanna was asked about his travels to Yemen in 2004 (the accounts Mehanna gave in that interview were false, according to the 2009 indictment). The primary aspects of those falsehoods were Mehanna's recollections of his interactions with Daniel Maldonado. Essentially, Mehanna was accused of lying to cover for Maldonado.

Upon Mehanna's 2009 arrest, the U.S. attorney for Massachusetts's press release offered a summary of these charges (Loucks 2009):

> Beginning in or about 2001 and continuing until in or about May 2008, **MEHANNA** conspired with **AHMAD ABOUSAMRA** and others to provide material support and resources for use in carrying out a conspiracy to kill, kidnap, maim, or injure persons or damage property in a foreign country and extraterritorial homicide of a U.S. national.
>
> Specifically, the Complaint Affidavit alleges that **MEHANNA** and co-conspirators discussed their desire to participate in violent jihad against American interests and that they would talk about fighting jihad and their desire to die on the battlefield. The Complaint further alleges that the coconspirators attempted to radicalize others and inspire each other by, among other things, watching and distributing jihadi videos. It is alleged that, among other things, **MEHANNA** and two of his associates traveled to the Middle East in February 2004, seeking military-type training at a terrorist training camp that would prepare them for armed jihad against United States interests, including United States and allied forces in Iraq.
>
> According to the Complaint Affidavit, **MEHANNA** and the coconspirators had multiple conversations about obtaining automatic weapons and randomly shooting people in a shopping mall, and that the conversations went so far as to discuss the logistics of a mall attack, including coordination, weapons needed and the possibility of attacking emergency responders. It is alleged that the plan was ultimately abandoned, because of their inability to obtain the automatic weapons they deemed necessary to effectively carry out the attacks.

This time line is of particular interest to me as Mehanna was my student in first-year composition classes in the fall 2000 and spring 2001 semesters, and again in the fall of 2001, that last semester in a detective fiction and film class. That semester, of course, was marked by the destruction of the World Trade Center on September 11, 2001. In that class, we read Raymond Chandler and Dashell Hammett. We watched *Chinatown*, *The Big Sleep*, and *Taxi Driver*. Here's one of the essay questions students could choose to respond to for their midterm:

> Joyce Carol Oates writes the following in regard to the hard-boiled detective genre: "The genre is a sort of demonic anti-pastoral in which 'laws' of probability are continually defied, and its primary truth of the human heart is that men and women, though more frequently women (if they are beautiful), are rotten to the core." Using the novel *The Maltese Falcon*, agree or disagree with Oates's claim and point out its larger implications.

Was it this semester that Mehanna became "radicalized" as his federal indictment asserts? Is it then that he discovered the power of language to reveal the human condition and foment revolution?

Mehanna's writing was a powerful feature of the no-longer-functioning website freetarek.com, allegedly maintained by his brother (also a former student at the Massachusetts College of Pharmacy & Health Sciences). Here's a poem Mehanna posted on January 13, 2010.

My Crime

> Here inside the dark side, every man has his crime
> For which he is responsible, for which he does his time
> Murder, rape, trafficking, stabbing, and assault
> They admit incarceration put their violence to a halt;
>
> But what is my crime for which I was snatched away
> And locked in a box painted pale blue, white, and gray?
> They pondered day and night over what shocking web to weave
> And in the end decided that what they want you to believe;
>
> Is that the reason for which I sit behind these cement walls
> Is: Terrorism! Assassinations! Weapons! And shopping malls!
> Flashback to when they stood before the entire world and lied
> Screaming "WMD!" to render a slaughter justified;
>
> If such could be done to fulfill that bloody vision
> What's one more deception to throw one man in prison?
> You might say there's no relation, but I'm telling you, my friend
> Is all part of an obvious & expanding trend?
>
> The crime for which the shackles squeezed & scarred my skin
> Is that I want the oppressed to prosper and to win
> The crime for which I was given this bright orange wardrobe
> Is the crime committed by innocents all across the globe!
>
> And my crime is my mind, uncolonized and free
> And that I am not the house slave they want us all to be
> And would not prostitute myself and agree to be of use
> To an agency that made my people the target of its abuse;
>
> These are my "crimes," for all to see and all to hear
> To which I plead guilty without hesitance or fear . . .

As I tried to make sense of Tarek Mehanna's plight and the role of writing and literacy in that outcome, I found particularly disturbing the writing that accompanied his case. In "news" accounts published regionally in the *Boston Globe* and nationally by major newspapers and websites, journalists largely parroted the federal prosecutor's charges and court filings, and often played into anti-terrorism hysteria and cliché. For example, on October 22, 2009, the *Boston Globe* announced above the fold on its front page, "FBI Calls Sudbury Suspect Inept but Serious Terror Plotter." In that article by staff writer Shelley Murphy (2010), we largely get the view of the indictment documents and the Department of Justice press release and follow-up press conference. We do get one paragraph of a statement from Mehanna's attorney and one sentence from his mother stating that her son "is a very good guy; he's innocent." Mehanna's mother, however, doesn't fare as well in a companion article titled "Records show man intent on terror, but supporters skeptical" (Valencia and Ellement 2009, A10). We're told, "His mother runs a licensed day care [out of her home]. State officials said that have had no day care-related complaints in the past, but will be looking into whether the setting is appropriate" (A10). We also get the now-routine view from Mehanna's Sudbury neighbors in this upscale suburb of Boston, where Mehanna lived in his parents' home. One neighbor tells reporters, "He was everyday normal. When he was out walking, he was friendly, neighborly."

As was true for Biswanath Halder, the always-disconcerting comment sections for online articles on Mehanna's case simply add to my dismay. To the *Metrowest Daily News* article by Julia Spitz (2011), titled "Who Is the Real Tarek Mehanna?" we get comments such as "I have an idea! lets shoot this guy at the firing line, if theirs really two, the good one won't die!" and "Julia I hope you showered after writing about this dirtbag." Conservative blogger Debbie Schlussel enters the fray to tell us, "Tarek Mehanna is yet Another Privileged, Homegrown Islamic Terrorist" and "another example of how Islam and its inclination to destroy us knows no borders or nationalities or socio-economic strata."

I would be wrong to assert that schooling and literacy did not matter to Tarek Mehanna. In the statement he read at his sentencing, he describes quite specifically those influences:

> When I was six, I began putting together a massive collection of comic books. Batman implanted a concept in my mind, introduced me to a paradigm as to how the world is set up: that there are oppressors, there are the oppressed, and there are those who step up to defend the oppressed. This resonated with me so much that throughout the rest of my childhood, I gravitated towards any book that reflected that paradigm—*Uncle Tom's Cabin, The Autobiography of Malcolm X*, and I even saw an ethical dimension to *The Catcher in the Rye*.
>
> By the time I began high school and took a real history class, I was learning just how real that paradigm is in the world. I learned about the Native Americans and what befell them at the hands of European settlers. I learned about how the descendants of those European settlers were in turn oppressed under the tyranny of King George III.

I read about Paul Revere, Tom Paine, and how Americans began an armed insurgency against British forces—an insurgency we now celebrate as the American Revolutionary War. As a kid I even went on school field trips just blocks away from where we sit now.

I learned about Harriet Tubman, Nat Turner, John Brown, and the fight against slavery in this country. I learned about Emma Goldman, Eugene Debs, and the struggles of the labor unions, working class, and poor.

I learned about Anne Frank, the Nazis, and how they persecuted minorities and imprisoned dissidents.

I learned about Rosa Parks, Malcolm X, Martin Luther King, and the civil rights struggle.

I learned about Ho Chi Minh, and how the Vietnamese fought for decades to liberate themselves from one invader after another. I learned about Nelson Mandela and the fight against apartheid in South Africa.

Everything I learned in those years confirmed what I was beginning to learn when I was six: that throughout history, there has been a constant struggle between the oppressed and their oppressors. With each struggle I learned about, I found myself consistently siding with the oppressed, and consistently respecting those who stepped up to defend them—regardless of nationality, regardless of religion. And I never threw my class notes away. As I stand here speaking, they are in a neat pile in my bedroom closet at home.

The years since Mehanna's initial conviction have certainly not been marked by increased tolerance for others, particularly those of Muslim faith. This assertion of values, born largely out of hate, fear, and ignorance, threatens not merely our Muslim neighbors but the very notion of a pluralistic democracy that we easily take for granted. To the federal government, Mehanna's First Amendment rights were certainly of far less importance than much hazier notions of protecting the United States from "homegrown terrorists." His faith in the power of reading and writing or his investment in a writing curriculum all his own, whether through his translation and posting of Arabic texts or his statements from prison, attest to an ongoing struggle to determine civic norms. That this struggle seemingly occurred far removed from the three writing classes in which Mehanna was my student tells me about the limits of schooling—and, ultimately, of reform. But what it also tells me is that a struggle over curriculum is often a struggle over much more significant issues than what students might choose to write about in first-year composition. Curriculum as an expression of values is fully bound with the struggle between education as a means of cultural reproduction versus cultural transformation. When writing is the particular tool for enacting that struggle, it makes a great deal of sense for writing teachers and scholars to pay close attention. The case of Tarek Mehanna is a story of the power and limits of the writing curriculum, particularly the limits of a writer's agency to bring about change in our world in the face of state power expressed via the legal and prison systems.

THE CURRICULUM OF WRITING AT THE END OF THE WORLD

In *Writing at the End of the World*, Richard Miller (2005) challenges readers to understand how, in his words, "might reading and writing be made to matter in the new world that is evolving before our eyes" (6). Just as Miller framed his discussion with examples of the Columbine high school shooters and the Unabomber, for whom writing did surely matter, so, too, does writing matter to Biswanath Halder and Tarek Mehanna. This mattering is perhaps not what Doug Hesse (2005) had in mind when, in his "CCCC Chair's Address," he poses the question "Who owns writing?" Hesse's assertion of our field's expertise in what he describes as "the knowledge of what writing is and what it can be, the whole of it, in every sphere" (355) is filled with possibility, though not necessarily of writers deciding just how, why, and when writing should matter in the extracurriculum.

Arguably, Halder and Mehanna "owned" a writing curriculum at critical moments, an ownership that has put both in jail for significant chunks of their lives. Both felt that the extracurriculum of writing was vital to create and would bring about justice, whether personal in Halder's case or more universal in Mehanna's. The state-sponsored curriculum of law and order, however, asserts its power, often through writing, with dire consequence for both writers. I certainly don't mean to justify the actions of either. Halder shot and killed an innocent man and terrorized many. Mehanna's intent to foment violence is far less clear, but I am not an attorney or a constitutional scholar. What I do know is that I knew both men, was their writing tutor and teacher, and their actions after those encounters can never be fully disconnected from the writing curriculum and pedagogy they experienced with me. For me, these two cases call into question the possibilities for and limits of our writing centers and classes and the ways that students' writing lives transcend the spaces our institutions often allow.

NOTES

1.   I take up the topic of writing center curriculum much more fully in chapter 7.
2.   For those involved other than Biswanath Halder, I am using pseudonyms to protect my colleagues' privacy.

PART 3

Empirical Inquiries

5

PRESTON SEARCH AND THE POLITICS OF EDUCATIONAL REFORM

The following is from the manuscript for Preston W. Search's *An Ideal School* (a passage that does not appear in the 1901 published version), page 94-B.[1]

Mr. Old Schoolman, who had come in early enough to hear a good part of the discussion, retired to his sleep that night to be greatly disturbed in his dreams by endless repetitions of A. H. Nelson's little poem, entitled "A School Idyl":

> Ram it in, cram it in;
>   Children's heads are hollow.
> Slam it in, jam it in;
>   Still there's more to follow—
> Hygiene and history,
> Astronomic mystery,
> Algebra, histology,
> Latin, etymology,
> Botany, geometry,
> Greek and trigonometry.
> Ram it in, cram it in;
>   Children's heads are hollow.
>
> Rap it in, tap it in;
>   What are teachers paid for?
> Bang it in, slam it in;
>   What are the children made for?
> Ancient archeology,
> Aryan philology,
> Prosody, zoology,
> Physics, clinictology,
> Calculus and mathematics,
> Hoax it in, coax it in;
>   Children's heads are hollow.

DOI: 10.7330/9781607328810.c005

Scold it in, mold it in;
   All that they can swallow.
Fold it in, hold it in;
   Still there's more to follow.
Faces pinched and sad and pale,
Tell the same undying tale—
Tell of moments robbed from sleep,
Meals untasted, studies deep.
Those who've passed the furnace through
With aching brow will tell to you
How the teacher crammed it in,
Rammed it in, jammed it in,
Crunched it in, punched it in,
Rubbed it in, clubbed it in,
Pressed it in, caressed it in,
Rapped it in, slapped it in—
   When their heads were hollow.

Understanding the promise and limitations of schooling often means making sense of a series of conflicts. There is the conflict between schooling as "an act of depositing," as Paolo Freire (1968) describes:

> Education . . . becomes an act of depositing, in which students are the depositories and the teacher is the depositor. Instead of communicating, the teacher issues communiqués and makes deposits which the students patiently receive, memorize, and repeat. This is the "banking" concept of education, in which the scope of action allowed to students extends only as far as receiving, filing, and storing the deposits. (72)

In contrast, is the notion of education as an active process of critical and creative knowledge construction. Another version of these contrasts is what John Dewey (1915) describes as "the difference . . . between having something to say and having to say something" (50). Further, in today's climate of high-stakes testing and barrier exams, there is the conflict between the imperative for measurable outcomes—and for institutions of higher education, favorable rankings in the *US News & World Report*—and the classroom as a creative, innovative space that meets the needs of all students no matter where they start or come from. These conflicts between efforts at reform and the persistent hold of the status quo, particularly in the ways they play out in English classes and writing assignments, are among the central narratives of the history of U.S. education, if not of the larger society, often cast as the struggle between ensuring individual freedoms and maintaining the communal good. Freedom and control also play out in the interplay between pedagogy and curriculum: do teachers have the freedom to alter pedagogical methods to meet students' individual needs? What is the effect of student-centered pedagogy when it is delivering a traditional or canonical curriculum? And how much curricular freedom is permissible when schools are faced with educating all students, no matter their level of preparation, motivation, or aspiration?

In this chapter, I offer a historical look at these tensions between pedagogy and curriculum through the experiences of one late-nineteenth-century educational reformer, Preston W. Search, who came to national prominence when he was superintendent of schools in Pueblo, Colorado, and championed in an 1894 article the "Pueblo Plan" of individual instruction. In the Pueblo Plan "the work is now conducted largely by what may be called laboratory methods. The entire time of the pupil is spent in active advance work. Every room is a true studio or workshop, in which the pupils work as individuals. The province of the teacher is not to line up the pupils and to consume time by entertainment, lecturing, and development of subjects; but to pass from desk to desk as the inspiring director and pupil's assistant, with but one intent and that the development of the self-reliant and independent worker" (157–58).

I first came across Search's concept of "laboratory methods" in my quest to find the first college-level writing center (Lerner 2009, ch. 1). It struck me then and now that Search's description of ideal teaching conditions—one-to-one instruction tailored to students' particular needs—echoes the rationale for writing centers as ideal places for learning and teaching writing. When I delved more deeply into Search and other reformers of his era, I learned that the 1890s, an era that historian H. W. Brands (1995) calls "the reckless decade," were a rich time for educational reform, at least when it came to pedagogy. In this ten-year period, public high school enrollments nearly tripled—from 22,000 in 1890 to 62,000 in 1900 (Snyder 1993, 34)—and educators, particularly in urban public schools, found that students, increasingly far more diverse in race, ethnicity, and preparation than previous generations, were particularly ill served by current teaching methods. Search's Pueblo Plan was an early attempt among many that educators offered to break the "lock step" (Washburne 1918) of mass instruction. As Carleton W. Washburne, an influential educator and writer from the San Francisco State Normal School, wrote in 1918, "Individual instruction must ultimately replace the lock step of class instruction because it is only by teaching <u>individuals,</u> that the time and material of courses can be made to fit those for whom they are intended. It is inconceivable that an inefficient, slow and harmful method of instruction should survive in the face of the proof of its evils. If the lock step is abolished, the only alternative is some form of individual teaching" (391).

By the time of Washburne's publication, Search was retired from public schools, living in Carmel, California, and plying the speaking circuit as the "Apostle of Individualism," offering lyceum-type lectures on "great ideals in life, history, literature, music, art" ("Preston W. Search" n.d.). Prior to this point, Search's attempts to reform urban public schools took him from Pueblo to two relatively brief appointments: as superintendent of the Los Angeles Unified School system from 1894 to 1895, and then as superintendent of schools in Holyoke, Massachusetts, from 1896 to 1898. Search was hired for both of these positions because of his national reputation as a reformer and his critiques of traditional schooling, and in both places Search was forced to resign as the result of political infighting, charges of profligate spending, and opposition to his ideas.

I offer the story of Preston W. Search as an example of the struggle for educational reform and the interplay between curriculum and pedagogy. While his educational ideas were not about teaching writing per se or directed at college-level schooling, Search's failures in Los Angeles and Holyoke are instructive in understanding the ecology of schooling, the many stakeholders who hold influence, and the resistance of the status quo to meaningful change, particularly when change results in increased student and teacher agency. While my main claim in this book is that writing studies needs to embrace its role in shaping curriculum, not just pedagogy, Search's story is also about the limits of pedagogical reform, particularly if curriculum is ignored or left intact no matter how inadequately it fits that particular population of students. Indeed, Search's ideas about curriculum were quite traditional. If anything, he pushed for delivering the college-preparatory curriculum of the time to all students, not merely the elite (a populist idea with its own set of controversies). In Search's 1901 book *An Ideal School*, his chapter on "the course of study" for high school students spends far more time on the need to distract boys, who "spend nine tenths of their time in thinking about matters pertaining to sex" (147), than on what the course of study might actually be. For that, Search describes quite conventional options: "The studies and media of the gymnasium or high school are choices in the sciences, grammar, Latin (and possibly Greek), French, German, literature, history, algebra and geometry, design, creation, play, gymnastics, music, and art" (151).

This conventional curriculum in the literal face of a nontraditional student body is one I return to in the next chapter, a classroom study of present-day Holyoke High School. In Search's experiences in Los Angeles and Holyoke, overhaul of instructional methods from "mass" to "individual" encountered resistance from parents, teachers, and school board members (unfortunately, I haven't come across the view of students themselves). The "grammar of schooling," as Tyack and Tobin (1994) describe the "regular structures and rules that organize the work of instruction" (454), is a powerful force to maintain the status quo. That the system of mass instruction and advancement by students' age, not by their level of mastery, largely holds sway today is testament to the challenges Search and other educational reformers faced. And I certainly cannot say that Search would have been more effective had he embraced the idea of curriculum being shaped by the students themselves rather than focusing on instructional methods to deliver a largely conventional curriculum. The forces working against Search's ideals were powerful in his era and in our present one. What Search's story does offer is one view of the real-world limits of educational reform and the ways "problems" of pedagogy and curriculum are far from solved.

WHO WAS PRESTON W. SEARCH?

Preston W. Search was born in Marion, Ohio, in 1853, was educated at the College of Wooster in Ohio, and also studied at universities in Lausanne, Switzerland, and Jena, Germany. At twenty-one, he began his teaching and administrative career back in Ohio as principal of the Millersburg Academy, but it was several years later, as superintendent of schools in Pueblo, that Search gained national prominence through his writing and speeches on what came to be known as the Pueblo Plan. As Search described it in an 1894 article, "the fundamental characteristic of the plan . . . is its conservation of the individual. The pupil is placed purely with reference to where he can get the most good for himself. He works as an individual, progresses as an individual, is promoted as an individual, and is graduated as an individual" (154).

While this description might not seem particularly radical today, in Search's era a focus on the "individual" was meant to counter the dominant practices of lecture and recitation and the associated march through a planned, textbook-driven curriculum with few or no adjustments for students' particular interests, strengths, or weaknesses. Search was not alone in his criticism of lecture and recitation as outmoded and inefficient means of instruction. In her book, *Impressions of American Education in 1908*, Sara Burstall, the head mistress of the Manchester High School for Girls in the UK, registered the following criticisms of recitation in U.S. high school English classes: "First, the possibility of what in England would be a probable waste of time to the listeners . . . Second, the whole thing is very dull and slow . . . Our third criticism is that the teacher appears to do too little; her share in the lesson is at a minimum" (1909, 157–58).

In an 1892 address, here's how Search described what he saw as dominant forms of instruction:

> Schools of absolute rather than of working order; of words, words, words; definition, definition, definition; abstraction, abstraction, abstraction; schools where the text book takes the place of the growing world; where the pupil gains all his information at second hand; where cramming and gormandizing take the place of investigation, appropriation and assimilation; schools where all is must and little of spontaneity; of examinations for the teacher's benefit, of ranking, of per cents, and other false rewards and incentives; of imitation, but no originality; schools that are for the masses and not for individuals; schools of high pressure, nervous tension and temporary results; of one-sided development, of precocity. (4)

In Search's Pueblo Plan, hands-on learning was key or, as Search (1892) described, "the new education teaches that 'activity is the law of childhood,' that all growth comes by activity and that in the school room nothing is to be so dreaded as passivity" (5). A key influence on Search was the "child study movement" of psychologist G. Stanley Hall, president of Clark University (Ludy 2006). For Hall, understanding children's needs and tailoring instruction accordingly were essential, and such study was "scientific" and "rational" as opposed to standard, teacher-driven methods of instruction. One hears Search echoing Hall's language in remarks he gave in 1895, noting that his plan for individual instruction "is scientific study with the child as the basis of the work. There can be no such study except by individuality" (411).

Also influential on Search's thinking, as on that of many educators at the time, was the work of Swiss educational philosopher Johann Pestalozzi and the belief that teaching children to discover and describe the natural world was essential to education (Search 1901, 4). The basis of these beliefs can be traced back to Jean-Jacques Rousseau, who believed that it was "natural" for children to be curious and want to discover and that schooling should be about freedom to learn, not mandated and repressive curricula (Search 1901, 4).

So what did this look like? In theory, at least, here's how Search (1892) described his methods:

> The new education presents to the student the ever-present and ever-growing world as the basis of study. The A, B, C's, of many departments

of study, the technicalities, the abstractions are banished from the school room work; while in their stead appear things, processes, growth, life. The text book with its many pages, its mechanical assignment of work and its iron-clad legislation is not allowed to arise like a great black pall between the inquiring mind and the world of beauty . . . The old-time recitation, which pre-supposes that the student must be dead an hour, and that many times a day, while the enthroned time-keeper and task-maker is checking up the class against dishonesty in previous preparation, shall be considered a relic of barbarism. (4)

Thus, for Search, the old practices that had seemingly served to educate the nation's elite conflicted with the new practices designed to serve all students, and as a result, the old had to go, the sooner the better. That is not to say that reform would ever be easy or wouldn't engender new conflicts. Search's experiences as superintendent of the Los Angeles school system are a case in point. That time was short because of a clash with city politics and educational "barbarism," one that would foreshadow Search's next stop as superintendent of the Holyoke school system.

FROM PUEBLO TO LOS ANGELES: LEFT ADRIFT ON THE LITTLE RED SCHOOLHOUSE FLOAT

Search left Pueblo (1890 population 24,558) for the position of superintendent of the Los Angeles (1890 population 50,395) school system, bringing his reforms for moving from mass to individual instruction to an urban school system that was growing rapidly. A September 18, 1894, *Los Angeles Times* article summarizing Search's inaugural address foreshadowed the tumultuous nine months that would follow as it offered the remarks of the speaker who introduced Search: "It is hardly necessary to say that in the establishment of great reforms in any department there is [as] a necessary result not only the sacrifice of much time and money on the part of the reformers but also the sacrifice of many personal friendships; such, I need hardly say, is our experience" ("Educational Ideas," 3).

Near the end of Search's first school year in Los Angeles, in April 1895, the American Protective Association (APA), an anti-Catholic, anti-immigrant movement, attacked Search for resisting their "Little Red Schoolhouse" float in the city's annual Children's Parade ("The Little Red Schoolhouse" 1895, 6). Several members of the city council and school board were open members or supporters of the APA and thus critical of Search. The APA seemed to take particular interest in schools, as demonstrated by an excerpt from a poem that ends their Statement of Principles, published in 1894:

> Noble men are in our ranks—
>> We are not a band of cranks–
> We are not a lot of bigots or of fools.
>> But, ye Roman Catholic hordes,
>> We will buckle on our swords,
> If you dare to meddle with our public schools. (Epstein 2000)

Direct attacks by the APA and its supporters were one front against Search. Another was the belief of school board members that Search's reform efforts were ineffective. As one told the *Los Angeles Times*, "They say . . . that Prof. Search is a great educator, of national fame and immense reputation. It can't be proved. The leading educational journals of the country are opposed to his system of instruction. It has been a failure wherever tried. It was a failure in Pueblo, and Prof. Search left that city because of that fact, and came to Los Angeles as a place hunter" ("How They Stand" 1895, 8).

Such broadsides did not directly cause Search to resign; instead, on June 21, 1895, the school board voted 6 to 3 to dismiss Search on the grounds that he had not established residency in Los Angeles at the time he was hired, regardless of the fact that his two predecessors also had not met this legal standard ("It Is Done" 1895). Two days later, on June 23, Search's public response appeared in the *Los Angeles Times*. "In this city I have had everything in my support, excepting the trading politician and the so-called American Protective Association, and they, by insidious manipulation have had the Board of Education and many good people misinformed. Is it possible, in enlightened America, and particularly in cultured Los Angeles, that such an outrage can be permitted to be perpetuated?" ("Hard Knocks" 1895, 12).

Clearly, the answer was yes. Search elaborated on the situation in "The Los Angeles Contest," which appeared in the first issue of the *Advance in Education*, a journal Search founded in 1895 "Devoted to the Conservation of the Individual in Mass Education, and the Essential Principles of Educational Unity." Search presents excerpts from Los Angeles papers to chronicle his dismissal by the board of education.

Los Angeles Times, April 12—A report was in circulation about the City Hall yesterday to the effect that certain representatives of the American Protective Association were about to attempt the removal of School Superintendent Search from office on technical grounds. The reason assigned for such a movement was that he declined to permit a representation of the "little red school house" in the Children's day fiesta parade.

Herald, May 18—Independent of the merits or demerits of individualism, it occurs to us that the fight against it is becoming a campaign against Mr. Search. It begins to look as though it might not be the defeat of this attempted innovation that is so ardently sought as the capture of Mr. Search's job.

Pasadena News, June 12—The opposition to Superintendent Search, which has been pronounced in the Board of Education of Los Angeles for some time, has resulted in the procurement of a legal opinion that he is not entitled to the office because he has not resided in the State and city for a year prior to his appointment. If this is good law, it would have been equally applicable to two of Professor Search's predecessors.

The Times, June 21—At its meeting last evening the Board of Education carried out the plan contemplated for some time and dismissed the Superintendent of Schools, Prof. P. W. Search. The pretext for his dismissal was that of ineligibility at time of his appointment, by reason of non-citizenship. The simple fact of the matter is, as *The Times* has heretofore pointed out, that Prof. Search was dismissed for other reasons than those put forward by the board as the cause of his dismissal, at last night's meeting. As will be seen from the report in another column, Prof. Search's friends were allowed to do all the talking, while his enemies had little to say. It was a case where silence on the part of the latter was indeed golden. (Search, "The Los Angeles Contest" 1895, 24)

Search then presented his conclusion:

Thus ended one of the bitterest fights in the history of American schools. In this contest more was gained than lost, for there will be three direct results to the Los Angeles schools: 1st. The Board of Education will make strenuous efforts to improve the schools in order to regain the favor of the people. 2nd. Even with return to the class method there will be more conservation of the individual then ever in the past. The body of individualism may lie buried, but its spirit will live on in the schools. 3rd. There will be an early change in the manner of electing members to the Board of Education, with removal of the schools from political despotism. ("The Los Angeles Contest" 1895, 26)

Unfortunately, Search was not particularly prescient when it came to "political despotism" in the Los Angeles schools, at least in the near term. Here's how his successor, Superintendent J. A. Foshay, began his summary report for the 1897–98 school year:

The school year 1897–8 will be memorable for tempestuous struggles in the Board of Education, resulting first in the dismissal of the superintendent of buildings for participation in a scheme for blackmailing teachers and employees, and later in the enforced resignation of one of the Board for the same cause, to be followed shortly afterward by another enforced resignation of a member for scandalous personal conduct. The struggle between decency and common honesty against indecency and corruption, extending over months and being attended with many sensational epi-sodes, was necessarily demoralizing to the school department; but, like the storm which devastates, it also purified the atmosphere and the schools to-day are on a higher plane, and there is a better tone among the teach-ers than there has been for years. (*Annual Report* 1898, 11)

Preston Search did not need to wait long for another opportunity to as-sert his ideas and run an urban school system.

SEARCH COMES TO HOLYOKE

In August 1896, Search was hired as superintendent of schools in Holyoke, which offered another urban laboratory to test his ideas for pedagogical reform. Holyoke was founded along the Connecticut River by Boston industrialists eager to exploit the force of the South Hadley Falls to power their paper and textile mills. Those mill owners filled their factories with immigrant labor—largely Irish and French Canadian in Search's era—to work the machines and make those owners wealthy. Here's how one writer described that scene: "In 1880, more than 3,600 textile workers who entered Holyoke's mills each morning comprised about half of the local work force. Six of every ten of these workers were women . . . Ten hours a day, six days a week, they performed the many operations necessary to transform raw cotton, wool, and silk into finished cloth" (Hartford 1990, 27).

The children of those mill workers, nearly 9,000 students, more than 70 percent of whom were from Irish and French Canadian families (Kidder 1989), filled Holyoke's public school system, and in Search's era, the rise and fall of Holyoke's great mills presented considerable challenges to the schools as enrollments grew but funding dwindled. In the words of one of Search's predecessors, describing the challenge in 1880,

Hundreds of these pupils, knowing not a word of English, enter our schools at the lowest grade. Some can read their mother tongue and know something of numbers, while others know nothing. While some have passed their thirteenth birthday, others . . . require . . . evidence . . . that they have passed their fifth. Differing widely in age, in degree of maturity, in home influences, in ante-school attainments, and of course in quality of character . . . agreeing in but one thing,—ignorance of the language—placed forty or fifty to a room at the beginning of a term, to be increased to sixty, seventy, or eighty within a few weeks, under one teacher, perhaps the last appointed and least experienced. (quoted in Green 1939, 288)

An announcement in the *Boston Daily Globe* makes clear that Search was hired in the interests of educational change:

> Preston W. Search, the newly elected superintendent of schools, will assume his office at once . . . It is stated that there will be many changes in the present condition of affairs. Mr. Search practically agreed to accept the office before he was elected [by the Holyoke School Board] . . . The members of the board say they will stand behind the superintendent in his reforms. One of the conditions of Mr. Search's coming to this city is that he is to be superintendent in reality. He is to have the entire management of the schools. He will probably be consulted before the list of teachers is appointed next year. ("Holyoke's Schools" 1896, 7)

The same news blurb gives an indication that not all, whether teachers or influential citizens, were happy with the school board's decision to hire Search. The article ends, "It is said that some of the teachers are seriously discussing resigning. The prominent citizens and heavy taxpayers, who asked that Mr. Kirtland [Search's predecessor] be retained, threatened to carry the fight into the municipal election this fall, when three of the school committeemen come up for reelection" ("Holyoke's Schools" 1896, 7).

In his inaugural address, Search described his educational ideas, making no reference to the events in Los Angeles or his potential detractors in Holyoke but instead looking ahead toward the possibilities for the Holyoke schools. Search did, however, offer one caution that presciently described what would be his relatively brief tenure in Holyoke.

> I have a definite knowledge of what I want to do; and now I shall expect full control of my schools and the earnest co-operation of all concerned. If I find in this community what I expect, the best energies of my life will be given to the up-building of a school system of the truest economy and, I trust, to the honor of Holyoke; but whenever the day comes in which I will be crippled in the execution of a live, vigorous and progressive policy, that day will bring the early severance of my connection with the schools. (1896, 88).

For Search, that day would not be far in the future. First, however, Search engaged in a successful effort to build a new high school, which opened in 1898. As Search described, "This school will stand for all that is best in the typical school, but beyond that it proposes to carry educational opportunity to young men and young women of every walk of life" (Holyoke School Committee 1897, 228). Indeed, Search's Holyoke High School was a clear counter to the idea of a training ground for the college-bound elite; as described by its principal Charles Keyes, it was not to be a school organized in terms of "the aristocracy who go on to college and the plebeians who cannot" (quoted in Green 1939, 305). Instead, the high school offered all students seven courses of study, including classics, modern language and literature, a Latin-scientific and English-scientific course, a business course, an art course, and a manual training course (Green 1939, 305). According to one account, "Each pupil was assigned to a section officer to direct him, conferences between pupil and teachers and teachers and parents were put into operation, and individual work in place of class work arranged. Visitors flocked to see the workings of this new model scheme" (quoted in Green 1939, 305–6).

For the high school English curriculum, the 1897 Holyoke School Committee report offers a quite conventional approach, with required readings from Addison's *Sir Roger de Coverley Papers* to Wordsworth's poetry. The two writing-related textbooks are *First Book in Writing English* by Edwin Herbert Lewis (1897) and *Composition and Rhetoric* by William Williams (1892). Both are conventional texts of their era, organized by modes of discourse and focusing on style as a process of building from words to sentences to paragraphs to themes. The emphasis is on "appropriate" expression, as Williams notes in his definition of "composition": "the art of finding appropriate thoughts on a subject, and of expressing them in suitable language and form" (1892, 5). "Appropriate" and "suitable," of course, are not determined by students themselves, no matter how "individual" the methods of instruction might be.

Despite his progress in Holyoke, in early November 1898, just into his third year as superintendent, Search offered his resignation, effective at the end of the 1898–99 school year. The *Holyoke Daily Transcript* ran a letter from Search headed "To the Citizens of Holyoke" in which he explained his reasons for resigning. Search opens his letter outlining the initial conditions of the system he agreed to run in 1896:

> The reputation abroad of Holyoke as a school city was not good.
>
> The city was divided by factional strife.
>
> The manner of appointment of teachers was bad.
>
> I had no time to throw away in any place where conditions were not right for progressive educational work. ("Mr. Search Resigns," 1)

After two years of relative harmony, Search had had enough. He attributed his resignation to being fed up with corrupt city politics affecting purchasing and hiring at the schools, as well as having received direct threats, such as the following letter: "Reinstate all the teachers dropped or expect the same treatment January 1. Holyoke will not tolerate such cruelty. If you do not at once comply with this request, you will be ripped up by the press. Signed, A Mill Owner" ("Mr. Search Resigns,"

1). After his experience with the American Protective Association, Search was no stranger to threats.

Later that year, the editor of the journal *School and Home Education* made note of Search's resignation and commented that

> in Holyoke, the politicians insist upon using the schools for personal ends, and employ corrupt methods in supplying school furniture and other supplies, while they refuse to equip the high school laboratory because some of the alderman have not yet been able to secure a sufficient rebate for themselves. ("Holyoke, Mass," 264)

I have yet to find angry letters from Search or his supporters in the *Holyoke Daily Transcript* or school committee reports of that time. Was the dissention a matter of Search's ideas for reform simply being too far ahead of what the city leaders might accept? Was it a matter of working within the severe financial constraints in Holyoke, still reeling from the Great Recession of 1893 and the overall economic slump in the paper and textile industries throughout the 1890s (Green 1939, 187)? According to historian Constance Green (1939), Search's resignation did indeed allow the Holyoke School Board to return to business as usual. She writes,

> Opposition to Search's program had been stirred up on the grounds of expense, but his policy of appointing the best teachers he could find regardless of their [place of residence] aroused consternation in the bosom of the old guard. The fact that his appointees were teachers of wide experience and unusual capabilities did not lessen local resentment . . . [After Search left,] the appointment of teachers evolved into a kind of patronage scheme for members of the School Board whereby each member of the board in turn had the privilege of nominating a candidate for a vacant position in the public schools . . . Where storekeepers and other persons anxious for public favor were members of the board—as was generally the case—the staff of the schools tended inevitably to be composed of persons having "pull" rather than exceptional qualifications as teachers. (308–9)

Upon leaving Holyoke, Search took his energy and ideas in a more public direction, going on the road as a lecturer and public speaker, studying under G. Stanley Hall at Clark University, and publishing a book-length description of his ideas for school reform, *An Ideal School*, in 1901. By 1914, Search had largely retired from public life and settled in Carmel, California, becoming active in local cultural events and other community work. In 1932, Search died from a stroke while visiting his sister in Riverside, California ("P. W. Search Succumbs to Stroke" 1932, 1).

THE LEGACY OF PRESTON SEARCH?

Nearly ninety years after Preston Search's death, it is likely that few in Holyoke or beyond have heard of him and his assertion of "individual methods." Is that because Search was too far ahead of his time, because his ideas for school reform seemed to be a solution in search of a problem? After all, for those who believe public education is working and always has been working, there is no reason to change. For those who think things are clearly broken, there is no power to create change. Search might have been a spokesperson for the latter, but as his experiences in Los Angeles and Holyoke attest, it is the former who are often in charge of city politics and educational policy.

Another complicating factor is that in the wash of history the problem often appears to be solved. In one 1932 obituary, admittedly a celebratory genre, Search is described as "the originator of the present system of city schools" ("P. W. Search Succumbs to Stroke," 1). If individual methods and learning by doing were the defining characteristics of city schools in the early 1930s, Search himself would have been quite surprised to hear it, as would subsequent generations of writers who have called for individual or "personalized" (Mickelson 1972) methods of instruction as a means of transforming education as we know it. The challenges of educating the children of immigrants at or below the poverty line in urban schools were not met in Search's era nor in our own. Tyack and Tobin's (1994) caution about educational reform is instructive here: "Reformers believe that their innovations will change schools, but it is important to recognize that schools change reforms" (478). The power of the entrenched status quo to resist reforms is often paired with a long-standing mistrust of students, an attitude that frequently appeared in critiques of Search's "individual methods" and the kinds of student freedom or agency he saw as essential to learning. For these critics, the essential role of schools is to instill discipline. In a review of Search's *An Ideal School,* Joseph S. Taylor (1902) writes that he can show "Mr. Search a school of 3000 pupils, where if this method of discipline prevailed, 500 children would spend their time in the yard playing marbles and shooting craps!" (166). Such "law-and-order" approaches to schooling, if not our larger society, will always be mistrustful of pedagogical and curricular reform. Change is indeed scary when the potential result is to put authority in the hands of students!

That's not to say that Search's ideas for individual instruction and student agency never took hold or cannot be seen in contemporary classrooms, particularly writing classrooms and writing centers. If anything, Search seems quite prescient in his published writing, recognizing the power of education if it meets students where they currently are, where they come from, and where they want to go. In an 1898 address, Search told his audience of teachers that "true education demands that the school shall fit the child and not require the child to fit the school" (421). Whether it's a focus on how students learn (e.g., National Research Council 2000) or current writing studies researchers' interest in students' transfer of knowledge (e.g., Eodice, Geller, and Lerner 2016, ch. 4), in our contemporary climate, Search's ideals have currency.

Whether they are translated from ideal into reality, however, is a process fraught with political, cultural, and educational obstacles, as Search's experiences show. Nevertheless, the pedagogical component—teaching practices targeted at individual students—is on the whole widely accepted (though admittedly unevenly applied). Reform of curriculum, however, is a much tougher nut to crack, particularly if that curriculum is to be co-created with students, as I call for in this book.

What Search's story offers writing studies is that pedagogy is as imbued with values as is curriculum and that reform of pedagogy is never enough, a particular challenge to counter those who believe the primary function of education is to "ram it in, cram it in." Any attempts at reform exist in the larger ecologies of schools, particularly urban public schools as central actors in conflicts of cultural reproduction on the one hand and cultural change on the other, all in the literal face of students who look and learn unlike previous generations. Search, ultimately, attempted to deliver a conventional curriculum by unconventional means to an unconventional student body, an approach that would be repeat around 120 years later, as I describe in the next chapter, a contemporary classroom study of one Holyoke High School teacher's efforts. In the mix of pedagogy, curriculum, and student agency in writing classrooms, the means to enact significant change remain frustratingly elusive.

NOTE

1.   A note about historical methods and data collection: my sources for material on Preston W. Search are his published writing as well as his papers kept at the University of California Berkeley Music Library. (Search's son, Frederick Search, was an American composer of note and donated his papers to UC Berkeley; his father's papers were also included in that donation.) Those two boxes of papers largely contain photocopied or original articles that had been published at some point, and I have cited those originals as print sources. The Search archives also contain a few of his memos written while he was in Holyoke, including two pleading his case to the School Committee to give him authority in hiring a manual instruction teacher (which the School Committee denied), as well as an original copy of his manuscript for *An Ideal School*, which I quote from at the start of this chapter. I also drew on Holyoke School Committee Reports, which include Search's inaugural address and are kept at the Holyoke History Room on the campus of Holyoke Community College.

6
LEARNING TO WRITE AT HOLYOKE HIGH

It's my first day observing in Ms. T's classroom, room 105 at Holyoke High School.[1] While Ms. T is in only her second year of teaching at Holyoke High, she comes to this school with experience teaching English abroad, and, before that, several years working as a journalist. I arrived bright and early on this March morning, the Friday after St. Patrick's Day, eager to start my three months of observation of Ms. T's five English classes: four British literature (three "standard" and one "honors") and one journalism, as Ms. T is also the advisor to the student newspaper. The day starts with homeroom: fifteen minutes of attendance taking, the Pledge of Allegiance, and announcements over the PA system. Some students sit with heads resting on folded arms flat on their desks; others read or stare into space. Everyone except me is wearing a picture ID badge hanging from a lanyard around his or her neck.

Holyoke High strikes me as an orderly place. In an urban high school in a rundown mill town in a school system that has seen 125 years of children of immigrants—first Irish and French Canadian, now Puerto Rican, Mexican, Cambodian, and Vietnamese —and where the Massachusetts education commissioner determined in 2015 that district-wide poor performance on state assessment exams meant the loss of local control and, as a result, the hiring of a "turnaround specialist," that order—or conversely, the lack of disorder—comes as a surprise. But order dominates, the halls completely clear of students while classes are in session except for a few teachers posted as hall monitors, quick to ask the occasional stray students just what they thought they were doing. That over four in ten students received an out-of-school suspension over the course of the school year that I was there certainly contributed to this sense of order (Massachusetts Department of Elementary and Secondary Education 2011b). There's little tolerance for disorder at Holyoke High, whether unauthorized roaming of the halls or more intellectual transgressions, such as plagiarism.

DOI: 10.7330/9781607328810.c006

The vice principal ends his announcements of meetings and deadlines with mention of the St. Patrick's Day just passed, an admonition to wear green on the following Monday, to make sure "the spirit continues." I look at these decidedly non-Irish faces around me and see no flicker of reaction. I suspect such admonitions are not unusual.

* * *

In his history of teaching English in U.S. public high schools, Arthur Applebee (1974) points to several "problems remaining," including

- "The acknowledged goals of the teaching of literature are in conflict with the emphasis on specific knowledge or content" (246);
- "Goals for the study of English depend upon prior assumptions about the nature and purpose of education" (252); and
- "The teaching of literature is a political act" (248).

In terms of the first two, Applebee points to the often-unstated assumption that "humanistic benefits would follow naturally from exposure to proper content" (1974, 246) but that the goals of teaching literature "are often in conflict and can be ordered only on the basis of principles which derive from assumptions about education as a whole" (252). The conflict between curriculum and pedagogy—particularly when it comes to teaching canonical British literature in an urban high school where most of the students are people of color—brings into sharp relief unstated assumptions about "humanistic benefits" and larger educational values and goals. The order of the school day in Holyoke High, accompanied by the largely traditional literature curriculum, speaks to assumptions about schooling as transmission of long-held societal and cultural values, or evidence of a "hidden curriculum" (Giroux and Purpel 1983). That such a traditional curriculum seems intended to instill certain kinds of "traditional" values in a largely nonwhite student body is one aspect of the "political act" that Applebee (1974) describes. He writes, "From the time of its use in colonial primers, the power of literature to shape values and beliefs has been recognized and put to use" (248). My observations indicate that it is not necessarily Ms. T's intention to transmit cultural values through the literature she assigns, but it is striking nonetheless how her students struggle to connect to what they read despite her emphasis on such larger themes as "good versus evil," "love and romance," and "heroism."

I did not come to Holyoke High with the intention of seeing the conflict between curriculum and pedagogy in action. As I described in the previous chapter, my interest in Holyoke started with Preston W. Search and his interests in educational reform. I came to present-day Holyoke to try to understand the legacies of Preston Search's efforts. What elements of student-centered education and individual methods would be present? What would the pedagogy and curriculum of the English classroom look like for majority minority students in a contemporary urban high school in a city struggling in yet another economic downturn? As I describe in this chapter, Ms. T's teaching of English emphasizes students' individual writing needs and attends to the processes of writing—pedagogical activities that would likely meet Search's approval. Meaningful curricular reform, however, is much harder to come by. The result for the majority minority students at Holyoke High of a traditional curriculum coexisting with contemporary "process" pedagogy is the experience of writing in school as a mostly dreary task, largely devoid of personal meaning and often disconnected from the meaningful writing they do outside of school. The pedagogy of student choice runs smack into the curriculum of canonical literature.

* * *

In 2010, 28 percent of all families in Holyoke and 44.6 percent of all citizens eighteen and under were living below the poverty line (U.S. Department of Commerce 2010), and Holyoke High is the primary high school for this urban community (Holyoke also has a vocational high school). Holyoke High qualifies for school-wide federal Title I funding, given the percentage of its students from low-income families. Additionally, the unemployment rate for Holyoke for 2012 averaged 10.1 percent, while the Massachusetts state average over that time period was 6.8 percent (Commonwealth of Massachusetts 2012). Despite these challenges, in 2010 Holyoke High had a four-year graduation rate of 74.5 percent (Massachusetts Department of Elementary and Secondary Education 2011b), compared to 67.2 percent for all Massachusetts urban school districts (Massachusetts Department of Elementary and Secondary Educationt 2011a). Of those students, 75 percent were attending college in the year following graduation, on par with the state average of 74.6 percent in 2008 (National Center for Higher Education Management Systems 2008). By these measures, Holyoke High is doing quite well.

The building Holyoke High occupies was built in 1964, and with its red brick exterior, low interior ceilings, and wide central hallways to manage the flow if its 1,300 students, it looks like many of the public schools built in the population boom of the 1960s. This "new" Holyoke High moved from the building that Preston Search had championed in 1898, heralded at the time as a "spacious new building equipped with fine laboratory facilities and with accommodation for eight hundred pupils" (Green 1939, 306). In Search's (1897) words, "This school will stand for all that is best in the typical school, but beyond that it proposes to carry educational opportunity to young men and young women of every walk of life" (228). After Holyoke High moved to its current quarters, the original building was occupied by Holyoke Junior (now Community) College. However, on January 4, 1968, the building was destroyed by "a general alarm fire of undetermined origin," according to a news account at the time (McSheffrey 1968). Today the area where the building once stood is largely an empty lot, bordered by Beach, Hampshire, Pine, and Sargeant Streets, a smattering of construction debris and parked cars filling the space where the high school once stood.

* * *

I was initially connected to Ms. T through the National Writing Project (NWP) site at which she had attended a summer workshop. Having been through two NWP Summer Institutes myself, I felt that teachers trained through the NWP would likely be strong and that what I would observe would not be a new teacher trying to find her way, but instead solid practices confronting the realities of urban public schooling. By and large, that is what I saw in Ms. T's classroom. She described her approach in an interview: "When I first started [teaching], I think I wanted to just make sure I covered everything. And then I started to realize that these kids didn't care, especially kids here in Holyoke. Because it's like they have so much that's going on at home, so much stuff going on in the community that I would never understand, and I am fortunate to not have to go through . . . It takes the task of teaching them, you know, like, if you wanted to teach them Chaucer, how does that work?"

Ms. T saw as her challenge the need to connect the required curriculum to what is relevant in her students' lives. As she told me at the start of my observations, "I found myself kind of going out on a limb and gearing my lessons according to the [required] frameworks, but also according to 'How is this going to tap into something that kids know about?' So that's probably one of the bigger things that I've learned in my six or seven years. I'm still new. [*laughter*] I'm still learning. I don't know anything. [*laughter*] That's the way it seems, you know."

Ms. T's British literature classes are part of the required sequence of English for all high school students. Whether standard or honors, the curriculum is largely dictated by state standards and is largely canonical, remarkably similar to Preston Search's era, albeit with a few more contemporary additions. Her British literature classes are described in her syllabus as follows:

In this course, you will become familiar with fiction, non-fiction, poetry, and drama from the different periods of British Literature. There will be vocabulary, lecture, reading, writing, discussion, group and independent work, and a research project. By the end of the school year, you should:

> Know the representative works of <u>all</u> major periods of British Literature between Anglo-Saxon times and the Twentieth Century.
> Know principal characteristics of a heroic epic, frame story, Medieval Romance, ballad, sonnet, Shakespearean drama, satire, and Romanticism. (This may vary slightly.)
> Know the historical and cultural premises that led to the origin of the English language.
> Recognize that the English language has undergone changes since its beginning.
> Recognize that historical and cultural developments frequently have influenced the writing of British Literature.

The literature surveyed runs from Anglo-Saxon to the Middle Ages to Victorian to the twentieth century. Students read *Beowulf,* Shakespeare, Spenser, Swift, *Jekyll and Hyde* and, at the end of the year, Lennon and McCartney.

Much of the writing activity is geared toward students' required research paper, for which students choose topics based on the literature they read. These standard literary analysis papers are described in Ms. T's syllabus as "3–4 pages + works cited page" for the "standard" classes and "5–6 pages + works cited page" for her honors section. While the assignment is perhaps not a burdensome requirement in terms of length, I noted during the time of my observations that many students struggle to find a topic, to include the required three references, and to invest effort into what felt like an extremely school-based genre and a task in which they saw little opportunity to express themselves or find meaning. Ms. T was not necessarily surprised by this lack of student engagement:

> I got a little concerned because of departmental questions during a meeting about like what are these requirements, and page numbers, and having to meet that department criteria. But at the same time like that department criteria seemed to be like wholeheartedly lacking to engage the students. Because it's like just writing a paper, and an analytical paper for the sake of writing an analytical paper. They're not going to get that, I know me, myself as a student, when a teacher would say do this, I didn't want to. I needed to know why, or I needed to have some sort of connection to it. And that's been the hardest thing because I'm not them, so I don't know what's exciting to them.

This is not to say that Ms. T's students were all reluctant writers or readers. During one of my visits, she introduces me to Zeda, a senior writing her research paper on the rich-poor divide in *The Great Gatsby.* Zeda tells me that she writes poems, song lyrics, or pretty much anything in her journal. Her writing allows her to express her feelings, her emotions, and she likes reading in order to understand another's point of view and "learn to be an adult." Zeda is the first of her family to graduate high school and is headed to the Marines. When I ask why, she tells me, "I'm tough," and that she decided to "stop complaining and do something about it."

Zeda's experiences are not unusual. On a "student writing attitude survey" that Ms. T asked students to complete before I visited, the sixty students who responded rated lowest on average the question "I wish I had more time to write at school" (2.2 on a 5-point scale) but rated highest on average the question "I like to read" (3.3 on a 5-point scale). The question "I like writing at school" received a decidedly middle-range response at 2.7 out of 5, while the question "I like writing notes and letters to people" averaged higher at 2.9. Finally, the question "I like to write" also received a somewhat middle-range response at 2.8 out of 5. In response to open-ended questions on the survey, a common theme is the motivation to write coming from personal interests, not necessarily from school assignments. In response to the question, "How do you feel about writing?" common responses include the following:

"I enjoy writing only when its something I want to write about."

"It's an okay thing. I do not like to do it all the time."

"It's okay depending on the topic."

"I think it can be fun if it's on a topic that is interesting."

"I like writing, especially when I have the creative space to do as I please with the words."

Whether the required literary research paper allows topics of interest and a "creative space" is debatable, according to some of the students. In one student's written reflection in response to "What do you wish you could change about your paper?" he wrote: "I would change everything, from the time constraint, topic selection to my paper itself. I was upset to find out we had to base our paper on a topic we covered this year. Nothing we read this year caught my eye and interested me, therefore the paper was aggravating. Also, to find out we had about two weeks to do it, it really upset me. It was two weeks that involved many, many projects and papers being completed. It was really hard to balance it all." I hear from other students who similarly see writing as a powerful tool of expression, but also as a school-based burden that rewards the trivial, routine, and mundane. Ms. T realizes these limitations, telling me in an interview,

Some of them don't like writing. And that's fine. I'm not here to make them love writing. I'm not the teacher that's like, "Oh, love writing. You'll all be crushed." Because I get it. "Oh, Miss, I can't write, I can't do this. I'm never good at this." Well, okay, if you're going to say that you're not good at it, of course not. Write me a paragraph. "Well, I'm stuck. I can't." And sometimes I would just ask them a question, and they'd explain it to me. And I'd say, "Okay, write that down." "What?" "Write it down." "Why?" "Because you just answered my question, and that's the continuation." "Oh." It's like they don't know. It just seems like the uncharted territory, like you're at the edge of the abyss. But you don't know that you can take a step, and somehow magically there's still ground there.

Ms. T's well-intentioned efforts to scaffold students' learning and build "choice" into her assignments are interpreted by some students as just another curricular requirement. Here's what Marco describes about his "feelings on writing":

> Well, I don't like to write much. I don't like to write about how I do the same thing everyday. I just don't see the point of that. If I write, I have to write about something special, something different, something that I think about a lot, or something I enjoyed. It can't be about how I walk everyday to school because that's just something I do on a daily basis. There's nothing special to that . . . When I do write, though, I do want to write very, very deep. I don't want to write how the sky is blue. I want to write about things that I enjoy. I want to write about how . . . Like, if I write about the sky for some reason, I would write about why it's blue, why I like it or dislike it. I would really get into it. I wouldn't just be like, "The sky is blue and there's clouds." I'm just not that type of person.

When Ms. T interviews Marco about the process of writing his junior literary research paper, he offers that he chose to analyze *Beowulf* because "I like the fact that he is a hero, that he is greater than everyone else. Just who he is, you know?" But Marco struggles to develop his topic, telling Ms. T, "I need to get some facts. I need to prove things, so I need to find some info and whatnot." She urges him to follow the use of sources that most of the other students similarly do: a primary text (the work itself they're analyzing), a dictionary as a secondary text to offer a definition of a key term ("hero" in Marco's case), and some additional secondary source to fulfill the requirement of three total sources. When Ms. T asks Marco how his paper is coming together, he replies, "It's all right, except I have a lot to do on it. I wouldn't say I'm struggling on it. I just have a lot to do on it."

* * *

Several students take up my invitation to record their literate lives outside of school by creating short videos with a Flip camera that I lent them. One group visits the Holyoke Mall, and in their video these students point out how they are surrounded by reading and writing: the logos on Wendy's cups, the directional signs in the mall, the text messages they are sending and receiving, or the job applications they are filling out. They narrate, "There's writing we need to read to tell where we're going." Another group records a drive through the streets of Holyoke, pointing out street signs that some pedestrians seem to ignore, all accompanied by a salsa soundtrack from the car radio. These students say, "You need reading and writing to get to where you're at," ending their video with "Reading is used everywhere; so is writing."

* * *

Ms. T manages to project outward calm for the great majority of the time. There are exceptions: she is perturbed by students who seemingly don't care, who float through their days with little ambition for taking advantage of the opportunities that Ms. T presents to them. And plagiarists. Ms. T is really ticked off by plagiarists.

Ms. T drags one such accused to a meeting with her and the vice principal. In the VP's cramped office, with various officious-looking notices pinned to the wall, the student slouches in a chair off to Ms. T's left, while she sits across the desk from the VP. What particularly annoys Ms. T about this student is that he is in her honors English class, one in which teenagers of relative privilege have decided to slouch and scowl their way through British literature from *Beowulf* to the Beatles. In the VP's office she lays out her case: the student had handed in his junior-year research paper with two unattributed quotes, even after Ms. T had flagged the need for attribution in previous drafts. The accused largely tries to blame Ms. T for her pedagogy, for not instructing him properly in the use of citations and for not giving him enough time to revise. In response, the VP stresses to the student the need to take responsibility for his actions and brings up the threat of suspension. The meeting lasts for less than ten minutes.

Back in the hall, the electronic bell rings three times in succession. It is time to start the next period, for Ms. T to return to her classroom and meet her journalism students, time to get to work on producing the school newspaper that will offer stories of athletic feats and opinions about the new lunch options and interviews with seniors about their plans for the prom. It's time for the halls to be cleared.

* * *

While plagiarists exasperate Ms. T, particularly when the culprits are her honors students, such behavior is simply emblematic of her of some students' larger lack of engagement with the curriculum or with the opportunities for learning that are represented in her classes. In our interviews, she described the problem:

This is my first year teaching an honors class, and . . . I kind of thought that this was going to be an okay class, it was talked up as this is going to be a class that's going behave, and do everything you want them to do, and I thought, okay, I guess I could deal with one of those classes. And all it turned out to be, the reality of it was sneakiness on the kids' parts with cheating, and plagiarism, and then not participating, but under the kind of guise that everything was too easy for them, to which my response was if it's too easy, you should still be able to answer it. And just a general shutting down of, you know, "She's making us do work." So it was disappointing, and it would seem as if the students would not deal with the issues at hand. They'd let a parent do it. Whereas the standard kids, there was apathy straight from the start, or it just seemed a little more real, like the kids wouldn't have their parents become involved, they would deal with it themselves, mostly because they're their own advocate, they don't have a parent to do that.

While Ms. T struggled to understand why her honors students might be disengaged from the curriculum (after all, they were "honors" students), she also found that their research, writing, and study skills were not particularly advanced:

I kind of assumed that [honors students] would have better research skills, and that they would be able to work faster. But from what I experienced they did not have that. And they didn't understand the concept of getting something done quickly. And that comes with time, but it definitely is required throughout college. These are all kids, like, if we were talking about the honors class, these are all kids that are going to go off to college. And I know that we haven't written a lot of papers this year, and that's perhaps why they might have been rusty. But maybe, I thought maybe if I had done something every month writing-wise, to build up to this, it would just, like a sport, you exercise, and you practice, and you get to the point where you can do it without thinking about it, or you're not as apprehensive, or you don't lose your resources, that makes sense. I really wished, and I really kind of want next year to be able to do more writing.

Despite Ms. T's regrets about not developing more fully her honors students' "habits of mind" about writing, she did spend a great deal of class time during my observations engaging students in freewriting on topics of their choice and in a creative writing/multi-genre project in which students had opportunities to write about "who they are and how they came to become those individuals" and, in Ms. T's words, find "multiple paths to literature." A major challenge, however, was connecting this project to students' required literary research papers when any apparent connections were not part of the curricular content.

* * *

Ms. T spent some time discussing with her F Block class what worked and what they did and did not learn from their literary research paper assignments:

> *Ms. T:* You can tell when it's done the night before, versus if you took time to do it. Plus you guys had all those middle checks, you know? Of like, "Did you do work today? Did you work today?" A lot of times kids wouldn't, okay? Or they'd try to pass off work from the day before. Because you guys put the date on it. What else? What else would you change? If you had the time, you would probably become more organized, you would use your time more wisely. L, what would you do?
>
> *L:* Nothing. [*laughter*]
>
> *Ms. T:* Huh?
>
> *L:* Nothing.
>
> *Ms. T:* Nothing? Would you do the paper? [*laughter*]
>
> *L:* Not really, I didn't hand it in.
>
> *Ms. T:* What impeded your handing it in? What made it not happen?
>
> *L:* I forgot my [thumb] drive at home.
>
> *Ms. T:* Drive?
>
> *L:* Yeah.
>
> *Ms. T:* Last one, what do you feel like you learned from writing your paper? Let's start with T, and then pick people out from there.
>
> *T:* What was the . . . ?
>
> *Ms. T:* What do you feel like you learned from writing the paper?
>
> *T:* I really don't know what I learned. Talk about timing, well, I'm not sure if I learned how to use my time wisely, but I sure did learn my lesson because of my grade. Well, I'm using your outline a lot for paragraphs and things, for essays, so I learned how to do an outline.
>
> *Ms. T:* Okay, that works. Good, pick someone else.
>
> *T:* L.
>
> *L:* I didn't learn anything.
>
> *Ms. T:* You didn't learn anything?
>
> *S:* You learned not to leave your geek stick at home? [*laughter*]
>
> *R:* It's called a geek stick.
>
> *T:* It is.
>
> *Ms. T:* Yeah. Well, that's a good lesson to learn, right?

* * *

Despite many pedagogical elements that Preston Search would recognize—student choice over topic (within the parameters of the assigned canonical readings, of course), attention to individual needs, Ms. T's efforts to have students connect literary themes to their experiences—students struggled with time and motivation. Once the papers were handed in and graded, Ms. T or I held discussions in each of her British literature classes for students to share their processes of writing their papers and what they felt they had learned. The most common outcomes were learning about time management (or lack thereof), about the play, story, or poem itself, about the particulars of citation format, and about the mechanics of using sources.

Certainly, these outcomes fit within the goals of the task and the curriculum, but they also seemed somewhat small; it was rare for any student to voice a learning outcome that described this paper and the process of writing it as meaningful in some way. But that's perhaps that nature of required and high-stakes writing tasks, ones that have choice in a certain way (students could choose any work of literature studied in class), but were limited in many other ways. In other words, the papers were primarily "the sky is blue and there's clouds" rather than "why it's blue, why I like it or dislike it." Ms. T reflected on these limitations in an interview, particularly the ways she felt her hands were tied by the required curriculum:

> Somewhere in that research, in that analysis process they all seemed to just fall by the wayside. I wanted to do more of like character analysis, or something where it wasn't so much theme based because I felt like a lot of kids, instead of it being, it turned into drudgery, and I did my best to not have it be drudgery. But still the stuff that I read was just boring, and I kind of wish that I could have opened it up to like, for instance, if someone wanted to write about the Beatles, like why not? Or if someone wanted to, there was an exercise in the book that I had found where they can invite four different characters to dinner, and that would be a character analysis. And I thought that would be kind of interesting too because it still would involve analysis, it still would involve citing from the play or the story or wherever. I wish there could have been more of a contemporary spin on it, you know.
>
> And I think that's why there were so many issues in the English class this year, especially the honors class, and maybe why I'd hoped more. Because that was the one class where they could offer their opinion and discuss and so something that was not, this is what you need to know, this, this, this. And I know it's going to be harsh to say, but I feel like they failed at that. Because I gave them the opportunity, and even after them not taking the opportunity I continued to give them the opportunity to discuss. Because every other class, history class is teacher directed, math class teacher directed, science class teacher directed. Whereas an English class can actually be student driven at times. And that's a gear shift, but at the same time I would think it would be a gear shift that would be likeable . . . because how do you not say your opinion? How do you not have a discussion?

That's not to say that I never witnessed in Ms. T's classroom the kind of opportunities to engage with writing that Preston Search would have approved of. In Ms. T's journalism class, students took on the tasks needed to put out a monthly newspaper with Ms. T acting as managing editor, circulating to offer feedback on students' writing in progress or to admonish some with "What are you working on right now? You need to find something to do." In many ways, students were creating their own curriculum, pursuing articles that they or their peers wanted to see in print. Taking on the role as faculty advisor to the newspaper was something that Ms. T particularly relished, and it was a familiar role given her previous work as a journalist. In her admission essay for a prestigious summer high school journalism institute (to which she was accepted), Ms. T wrote,

> I remember the exact moment when I chose to become my inner-city high school's journalism adviser. It was last year on a sweltering afternoon in June. I was walking back to the room that I shared with a fellow teacher when I passed the "newspaper room." The teacher who started the year as adviser had quit after the first semester and a long-term substitute had taken over the classes. The lights were off and inside were a handful of students looking bored or surfing the Internet. Our school already didn't have very many electives and this class had so much potential. The thought bubbled up: take a chance and change it . . .
>
> Seven months later, my staffers and I have become a team. We promised from the first day of class to learn from our mistakes, communicate, and always meet our deadlines. We've published two issues that have made our class, our school, and our community very proud. My staffers have become more media literate and now further understand the power of the press. With a minority population of 68%, our inner-city school is marked as failing and hopeless. Still, my staffers don't see it that way. They are giving our school a voice to report on the positive things happening here and in our community. My staffers show me on a daily basis that they are not just earning credits to graduate. They show me that they are thinking and pushing the boundaries, all the while learning about a future career and how to be a responsible citizen who *can* uplift their community.

Ms. T and her journalism class, however, were producing that paper in a particular school-based context. Throughout the semester, I see Ms. T clash with school administration over putting the paper online and over the paper's content, particularly an April Fool's issue, which reported that Holyoke Mall would close, putting many teenagers out of work. That was a too-close-to-reality circumstance on which the administration put the kibosh. As Ms. T told me in an end-of-term interview, "When the April Fool's edition of the paper didn't come out, that just totally crushed that class beyond repair."

On my last day of observing Ms. T's classes in the middle of June, once again the day starts with homeroom, announcements over the intercom, and the Pledge of Allegiance. It's quiet as students stare into space, chins resting on their hands. The electronic bell rings three times, and students quickly exit for their first-period classes, or "A Block." Later, in Ms. T's British literature class, she offers students the opportunity to connect their personal experience to what they would be reading, asking them to write in their journals how they would respond "if someone wrote a song for you." She recommends, "Be thoughtful." She then adds, "Six to eight sentences for full credit," a familiar reminder that choice and expression are bounded by requirements.

* * *

I like to think that a progressive such as Preston Search would find much to admire in present-day Holyoke, particularly in its grassroots efforts to reform city politics. In 2011, Holyoke citizens elected as mayor Alex Morse, twenty-two years old and openly gay, a graduate of Holyoke High School and Brown University, the first of his family to graduate from college and the first Holyoke mayor to be fluent in Spanish (Luthra 2012; Powers 2012). Morse's defeat of the sixty-seven-year-old incumbent marked a new era for Holyoke, though one account of Morse's first six months in office noted that he was challenged by "the City Council, filled with entrenched political families, [which] has historically held significant power" (Powers 2012, A1), an urban reality that Preston Search would surely recognize. Morse has since been reelected as mayor twice, most recently in 2015.

Search, too, would likely recognize the teaching practices common in Ms. T's classroom: an emphasis on activity, on creating opportunities for students to make meaning, on Ms. T's individual attention to students' needs. While her English classes might have been an exception to the students' overall high school experiences (as Ms. T indicated in an end-of-term interview), they still offered opportunities for learning that Preston Search would have likely approved, and it would not be inaccurate to say that such practices are to be found in high school English classes nationwide. While elements of long-standing "current-traditional" approaches surely abound (Berlin 1987, 36–43), the writing process movement, now more than forty years old, has made its presence felt in writing classrooms from kindergarten to college (Applebee and Langer 2011; Matsuda 2003). Indeed, what strikes me now about what I saw in Ms. T's classroom during my weekly visits is how completely familiar it all felt—not particularly different than my own suburban New Jersey public high school experience in the mid-1970s and consistent with process pedagogies in force for multiple generations of students. The amount of writing Ms. T asked her students to produce during the period of time I observed her classroom is also in accord with what Applebee and Langer (2011) have reported as typical for high school English classrooms in their national study of writing instruction (15).

Nevertheless, the familiar feel of Ms. T's classes belies the fact that Holyoke High's students are not traditional. The majority minority, multilingual population studying nearly the same literature curriculum as was prescribed in Preston Search's era is but one example of a disconnect between a traditional curriculum and nontraditional student population. While Ms. T did have her students try to connect their experiences to the larger themes of the literature they were reading, most opted for traditional topics when it came to their writing. It was not even that Ms. T enforced traditionalism (for example, one student chose to compare Sir Gawain to comic-book hero Ironman), but somehow the traditional route is the one that most student chose, despite their potential lack of interest in the topic. It was a safe path, one signaled by the textbook they were using, by the official school curriculum, by years of standardized testing, by generations of Holyoke High students preceding them. For the teaching of English in contexts such as Holyoke High, notions of the "translingual" classroom (Horner et al. 2011) where language use, its politics, and its power are the curriculum offer exciting possibilities. But those possibilities are seemingly thwarted by many factors that limited what Ms. T could accomplish in her classes, whether required tasks, state-mandated assessments, or any teacher's reluctance to offer resistance to entrenched practices, particularly when that teacher is relatively new, relatively low in the hierarchy, and from a different racial, ethnic, and social class than most of her students.

* * *

Perhaps the best-known teacher in Holyoke is Mrs. Zajac, a fifth-grade teacher and Holyoke native in one of the city's elementary schools described in another study of teaching and learning in that city—Tracy Kidder's (1989) *Among Schoolchildren*. Kidder writes, "Decades of research and reform have not altered the fundamental facts of teaching. The task of universal, public, elementary education is still usually being conducted by a woman alone in a little room, presiding over a youthful distillate of a town or city. If she is willing, she tries to cultivate the minds of children in good and desperate shape. Some of them have problems that she hasn't been trained even to identify. She feels her way. She has no choice" (53).

In December of the year I observed Ms. T's classes, she sends me an email, asking if she could put me down as a reference as she applies for new jobs. "Nonteaching jobs?" I ask. "Yes," she says, "it's been a stressful year."

Ms. T stayed at Holyoke High one more year, but as the following fall approached, she decided she had had enough and resigned her position, joining the more than 40 percent of public school teachers who leave the profession within their first five years (Ingersoll, Merrill, and Stuckey 2014, 23). Today she's back to working as a journalist and an artist. Ms. T's time in Holyoke was three years, matching exactly Preston W. Search's tenure as superintendent. For these two educators fully committed to their students' futures, I can say with confidence, the challenges of educational reform are a complex reality.

NOTE

1. A note about methods of data collection for my research at Holyoke High School: I was a true participant observer in Ms. T's room. I kept observational field notes and interviewed students individually and in small groups. Ms. T also had me participating, whether contributing to class discussion or conducting one-to-one writing conferences with students as they worked on their required literary analysis papers. Further data collection was enabled by our use of Flip video cameras, whether it was Ms. T recording her individual writing conferences with students and her whole-class reflection/discussion on students' processes of writing their literary analyses, or students borrowing the cameras to tell me about and document their out-of-school reading and writing practices. In addition, I asked students to write reflections on what they learned from doing their literary analyses, which I collected. Finally, I conducted forty-five-minute interviews with Ms. T at the start of my observations and at the end of the school year, and had frequent email exchanges with her both during and after the period of time I was in her classroom. The use of "Ms. T" is intended to protect the privacy of this teacher; all students' names are pseudonyms.

7

THE HIDDEN CURRICULUM
OF WRITING CENTERS

While the previous chapter reports on a visible intended curriculum in high school literature classes, in this chapter I take up a curriculum that's far less obvious: the curriculum present in writing center sessions. Having served as writing center director at two different institutions and having been involved in the field as a tutor, researcher, scholar, and professional for over thirty years, I see the liberatory possibilities of a writing center curriculum often in conflict with the normalizing functions of writing center work. However, that this conflict is curricular is, in and of itself, a perhaps unexpected way of viewing what happens in a writing center. Elizabeth Boquet (1999) describes writing centers as occupying two separate—but potentially overlapping—spaces: one pedagogical, or the writing center as method, and one physical, or the writing center as site (464). Both configurations largely capture the history of writing centers in U.S. higher education, whether those sites have been conceived of as writing laboratories and clinics in various eras in which students were sent to have their "deficiencies in writing" fixed or whether writing centers have been viewed as safe havens of sorts, distinct from classrooms with their mass education approaches and nonindividualized instruction. Writing center pedagogical approaches stress the power of one-to-one instruction, of entering the "Burkean Parlor" (Lunsford 1991) for rich conversation and knowledge building around students' texts and interests. These pedagogies do not need to be contained within the (basement) walls of the writing center but have the power to spread the word, in a way, whether via programs that assign tutors (usually undergrad) to specific classes (Zawacki 2008) or when the writing center might act as a leader on campus for its innovative approaches to learning and teaching.

Writing centers do not have a curriculum in the traditional sense—there's no curriculum committee that has approval over syllabi that a writing center submits, no specific learning goals or outcomes that writing centers commit themselves to meeting (though this is slowly changing in response to assessment demands). Nevertheless, the

DOI: 10.7330/9781607328810.c007

curriculum of writing centers was present in the work I did as an MA student at San Jose State University in my first foray into writing center work, and is present in every session, face-to-face and online, every workshop, every communiqué from the writing center to the outside world.

One example of writing center curriculum—and of curriculum as an expression of values—can be found in the ubiquitous claim in writing center practice that "we don't proofread, but we'll help you learn to edit your own writing." While this response seems largely about pedagogy (how we'll tutor and how we will not tutor), it does assert curricular values that proofreading is the domain of the individual writer, not the writing center, that the goal is for students to learn to do the writing/editing/revising/proofreading, not for the tutor to do these tasks *for* the writer, that successful writers do not rely on others for proofreading, that proofreading is a somehow tainted practice and that asking others to do it is to reveal oneself as false—not a real writer or one with intentions to cheat. The moral/ethical dimension of "we don't proofread" asserts writing center curriculum as cultivating "honest" work and guiding student writers down a virtuous path, one in which they would never again ask someone to do the work they rightly should take on themselves. Further, the "we don't proofread" mantra asserts a specific definition of proofreading, one that student writers might not share, creating a clash of curricula (for student writers do bring a curriculum to every session, one that is likely even less fully articulated than the curricula the writing center represents). Further, the curriculum of "we don't proofread" positions tutors as gatekeepers, approving or disapproving of students' attempts to set the agenda of sessions. It asserts clear roles, then, for tutor and student, and these roles have curricular substance. My claim in this chapter is that much of the curriculum of a writing center is hidden from view or assumed to be shared. The result is a potential mismatch of expectations and outcomes, and this discordance is a contributing factor to the persistent marginalization of writing centers in the higher education landscape.[1] By articulating their curriculum, not merely their pedagogy, writing centers have the opportunity to name what they know and who and what they are, and to assert expertise in ways that might just lead to the kinds of leadership roles on their campuses that seem to have been elusive for the last thirty years. And beyond campus leadership, writing center studies as a disciplinary construct, as is true for writing studies as a whole, is impossible without a clear articulation of curriculum. Aspirations for writing center scholarship to be taken seriously will not come from mere application of research methods, such as those that are RAD (replicable, aggregable, data supported; see Driscoll and Perdue 2012; Haswell 2005a), or from claiming ownership of one-to-one pedagogies (Lerner 2014), but also from articulation of curricular content.

To move toward that articulation, in this chapter I report on research concerning the events of day-to-day tutoring, the interactions of tutors and student writers. While one might argue that the curriculum in these instances is supplied by whatever task the student writer is bringing to the session—whether biology lab report, first-year writing narrative essay, or resume—my claim is that the ways that tutors and writers interact with these tasks and with each other asserts a curriculum. In this way, curriculum is not merely content but instead a product of the interaction between tutors and writers as well as that content (and, of course, with influences not immediately present in that session, such as each instructor's and participant's history with tutoring and writing or the short- and long-term goals and values that both bring and, at times, articulate). This social dynamic is not a new concept, given the long-standing social-epistemic focus of composition studies. However, the consideration of writing center work as fully social is more than an articulation of "tutoring as a social process," as Ede (1989) and Lunsford (1991) stressed many years ago, but instead a recognition that amid the social dynamics of tutorial interaction, a curriculum is a continually constructed, present, and driving force.

To investigate that force, in what follows I offer an analysis of tutorial interaction, focusing on those moments when tutor and student writer come together to assert the curricular basis of the writing center. While my methods in this chapter are quite different from the rest of the book—here I rely on qualitative coding and quantitative analysis of results—my intent in employing these methods is not only to account for the hidden curriculum of writing centers but to highlight the curriculum that is present in every literacy event, no matter the context. As I've stressed throughout this book, curriculum is an expression of what we value when it comes to learners, teachers, learning spaces, and subject matter, as well as of the complex interactions of these elements. A view of the curriculum in a space largely seen as pedagogical—a university writing center—offers both research methods and implications for viewing curriculum in any site of literacy learning.

METHODS AND DATA FOR STUDYING
WRITING CENTER CURRICULUM

The tutoring sessions I analyze in this chapter took place at a medium-sized private university in the northeastern United States.[2] That university's writing center employs a mix of undergraduates, master's students, and PhD students as writing consultants. It also contracts with WCOnline (https://mywconline.com) to provide scheduling software and a platform for synchronous online tutorials, and it is a selection of these online tutorials that constitute my dataset. As shown in the screen shot in appendix B, the online tutorial task environment includes a space for students to upload their written work and their assignments and a chat box for real-time conversation between consultant and student writer about the student's project. The tutor-writer conversations in the chat box constitute the data I present in this chapter. I chose that data source for several reasons:

1. I had access to these online sessions.

2. The archived chat eliminates the need for audio or video recording and transcribing.

3. A focus on tutorial chat transcripts eliminates to some degree the many variables that might constitute curriculum in face-to-face settings, particularly nonverbal communication such as gestures, body positioning, facial expressions, or other means of expression.

The chat transcripts that constitute the data for this chapter come from twenty online sessions in the first week of October in the fall 2016 semester. My choice of this time frame was mostly guided by the knowledge that the writing center would be fairly busy by that point (approximately week 4 of the semester; these twenty online sessions were 16 percent of all sessions held); thus, I'd have an opportunity to capture data. The online sessions were conducted by fifteen consultants working with nineteen different writers.

Before coding, I removed names of both consultant and student in each session, substituting "Tutor #" and "Student #" for real names, starting with the first session that week and ending with the twentieth.[3] To do the analysis, I saved the chat from each session as a .txt file and uploaded it to HyperResearch, v. 3.7.3, as "cases" (http://researchware.com). My research assistant and I then worked with a small sample of sessions to reach agreement about coding categories, had another discussion after my "audit" of her coding about three-quarters of the way through the corpus, and then talked extensively about transcripts.

In terms of coding transcripts for curriculum, my focus was on three kinds of knowledge claims: (1) role knowledge, (2) writerly knowledge, and (3) emotional knowledge. My premise is that assertions of these types of knowledge from either tutor or student constitute a writing center curriculum, as I next describe.

Role knowledge: Articulated claims about the roles tutors or students might play or that they expect their interlocutor to play have a strong effect on the interaction itself, whether to propel the session along if those roles are accepted by each participant or to create tension and potential conflict if those roles are not accepted. By assuming particular roles, tutors and students are asserting particular norms for the session, and these sociolinguistic features carry from one session to the next. These behavioral patterns are curricular in nature in that they represent knowledge about how to interact in the genre of the tutoring session in order to accomplish one's goals. In classroom settings, the roles that students and teachers assert through their interaction are often seen as one example of the "hidden curriculum" (Giroux and Purpel 1983). For example, the students sitting in rows, raising one's hand before being acknowledged by the teacher to speak, not interrupting another classmate—all convey a strong social curriculum of order and authority. Another example of the hidden curriculum of teacher and student roles is the common initiation-response-evaluation (IRE) pattern of interaction (Cazden 2001). In these cases, the teacher initiates an interactional sequence with a question ("What's the capital of Wyoming?"), a student responds ("Laramie?"), and the teacher evaluates ("No, that's wrong, Franco. It's Cheyenne."). The knowledge of who talks when and what's acceptable to say contributes to student learning not merely about the topic of the conversation but about the social rules of interaction. Similarly, tutors and students bring to each session knowledge about the roles each should play and express that knowledge through language, whether spoken or, as in this study, written.

Writerly knowledge: I label as "writerly" knowledge those instances in which tutor or student expresses a claim about how writing, writers, or the writing process should work. These are ideally common utterances in writing center sessions, whether face-to-face or online, as tutor and student express an evaluation of the student's writing (often in response to a question), the student describes her writing processes, or the tutor offers advice on revision strategies.

Emotional knowledge: Conversational turns that I coded "emotional knowledge" feature instances in which tutors or students offer empathy for their interlocutor, express support, commiserate, or in some way connect on an emotional level with one another, an outcome of writing center tutoring that has long been valued (e.g., Harris 1995). Thompson (2009) describes these instances as a tutor performing "motivational scaffolding," which is characterized by "acknowledging that the task is difficult; using humor; providing negative or positive feedback;

reinforcing correct responses from students by repeating them; helping the student maintain motivation and control frustration through sympathy and empathy" (428). While Thompson was examining only tutors' verbal actions, I include both student and tutor utterances of emotional knowledge to capture the interactional nature of these responses.

The results that follow and their demonstration of the curriculum of a writing center as expressed via tutorial discourse offer empirical evidence of several long-standing threads in writing center literature: directive versus nondirective tutoring, student-controlled agenda versus tutor-controlled agenda, higher-order concerns versus later-order concerns, and a focus on the writer versus a focus on the writing.

CURRICULAR RESULTS: TUTOR AND STUDENT KNOWLEDGE CLAIMS

Figure 7.1 presents the most frequent tutor and student knowledge claims or assertions of curriculum in terms of role knowledge, writerly knowledge, and emotional knowledge. Regarding the total number of claims over the twenty sessions, tutors were more likely than students to offer knowledge claims, a statistically significant difference. In terms of particular types of claims, tutors were more likely to make claims about roles and writerly knowledge (the latter a statistically significant difference), while students were more likely to make emotional claims than were tutors (also a statistically significant difference). These results point to tutor dominance in these sessions in terms of total claims and role knowledge and writerly knowledge. In other words, tutors talked more than students when it came to these two types of claims, as well as for all claims.

Of the three types of claims, role knowledge was the most likely to occur, making up 63 percent of all tutor claims and 65 percent of all student claims. Thus, in these twenty online sessions, tutoring writing was much more about the relationships between writers and tutors as they negotiate what each should do and how each should interact in a session.

A more granular look at tutor and student knowledge claims is shown in appendix C, along with examples of each claim. I next describe these findings according to role knowledge, writerly knowledge, and emotional knowledge:

Role knowledge: The most frequent tutor role knowledge claim was to suggest changes, and the most frequent student role knowledge claim was to express thanks, usually in response to those tutor suggestions for

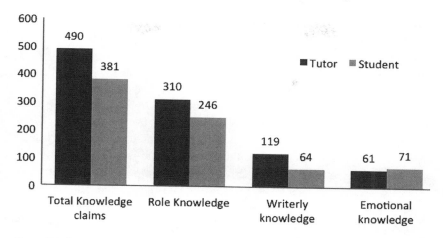

Figure 7.1. Frequencies of tutor and student knowledge claims. Differences between tutor and student total knowledge claims, role knowledge claims, and emotional knowledge claims are statistically significant at $p < .05$.

change, and, as I pointed out above, these role knowledge claims occur far more frequently than any others.

Tutors' role knowledge claims position them firmly in charge: suggesting revisions, offering feedback, managing time, dispensing knowledge about the use of the WCOnline interface, among others. Students' role knowledge claims often position tutors in these specific roles while students' roles, other than to give thanks, are to offer context for their writing task and to assure tutors that the feedback they offered was helpful. Of particular note is that the role of agenda setting, a topic of a great deal of attention in tutor-training scholarship (e.g., Newkirk 1989), does not figure prominently in these findings, occurring 2.8 percent of the time for students and 2.6 percent of the time for tutors.

Writerly knowledge: For tutors, nearly one-quarter of all writerly knowledge claims consisted of sharing genre knowledge, whether about essays in first-year writing or personal statements for graduate school applications. Tutors once again are performing as "experts," holding specific genre knowledge that they dispense to students. Other than genre knowledge, the writerly claims that tutors make are dominated by issues of clarity, issues of what I would label "essayist" literacy (e.g., coherence, thesis statements, introductions and conclusions), and language-level concerns (e.g., language correction). For students, writerly knowledge was dominated by attention to organization, argument, and response to their writing prompt or the expectations of their professors. These areas of focus speak strongly to the school-based tasks and context for these sessions and largely instrumental writerly actions on both tutors' and students' parts. In other words, it was rare to see a kind of writer-to-writer talk, idealized in much writing center literature as a rich conversation in Kenneth Burke's academic "parlor" (e.g., Lunsford 1991).

Emotional knowledge: Tutors offered only three kinds of emotional knowledge claims, and most frequent by far was to offer students validation or affirmation for their efforts. Coupled with these responses were students' most frequent emotional knowledge claims: to offer self-doubt, fear, or anxiety about their writing or the emotional context for what they had brought to their sessions (e.g., anxiety about the task itself). In these claims, one can see a writing center session as an opportunity for students to express the anxieties and fears that are all too common when it comes to school-based writing tasks.

Another way to look at these data is by what kinds of particular knowledge claims occurred most frequently for tutors and students. As shown in tables 7.1 and 7.2, for both participants, role knowledge dominated and writerly knowledge was relatively rare—and when it did occur, for tutors it was an expression of genre knowledge and for students it was about the organization in response to a writing prompt. Emotional knowledge most frequently involved tutors offering students validation or affirmation and students expressing doubt, anxiety, and failure.

As a way to enact these claims, what I offer next is a manufactured dialog of a tutoring session, drawing examples of most frequent knowledge claims from seven different students and seven different tutors. Note that the session starts and ends with what I label "shared role knowledge" (ShRK), the exchange of greetings or pleasantries that opens and closes most sessions. In parentheses after each kind of claim is its frequency in the overall data set:

> *ShRK*: *Greetings/exchange of pleasantries is appropriate way to start. (24)*
>
> *Student 4*: hi!
>
> *Tutor 4*: Hi Student 4! I'm Tutor 4, your WC tutor today.
>
> *tRK*: *Tutor's role is to query student to set agenda. (23)*
>
> *Tutor 8*: So what can I help you with today?
>
> *sRK*: *Student's role is to provide context for the writing. (24)*
>
> *Student13*: Hi, Can you see my typing? I hit the enter after I typed but it didn't go Yes, I'm in Beijing now, I need to use VPN to connect myneu I am going to apply for another school . . . I don't want to be stage manager anymore I'm not happy working in Beijing Did

you receive my personal statement? I did the first draft Yes I did Yes, please I want to revise some grammars and I am not sure if my personal statement is good enough for business major Thank you!

tRK: Tutor's role is to explain use of online tools. (25)

Tutor 10: you can 'copy and paste' it on to the board

sRK: Tutor's role is to assess quality of student revision or proposed revision. (33)

Student 14: this is the first part of my answer to the question; could you please read and give me some feedback?

tRK: Tutor's role is to suggest changes. (54)

Tutor 13: Again like we mentioned earlier you could shorten the beginning a little bit, especially once you write a more appropriate introduction. If you have to cut I believe the first paragrp oh you have now could easily be shortened.

sRK: Student's role is give tutor affirmation. (25)

Student 2: Thanks for your feedback. I think it was actually helpful.

tEK: Offer validation or affirmation. (40)

Tutor 4: Your experiences are what make you special and they inform your future

sRK: Student's role is to be thankful. (42)

Student 19: thank you for your help. I am going to try and get this down so my assignment is done next time.

tRK: Tutor's role is to praise student. (28)

Tutor 15: ok thats actually a good start! i've helped many people who didn't have any articles to begin with haha

sEK: Express self-doubt or uncertainty. (19)

Student 17: and I am not confident about the introduction and conclusion

tWK: Genres have particular requirements or features. (28)

Tutor 10: well, it depends on genre: in a "narrative" the conclusion will usually express something very different from the beginning because it is the end of whatever development/ journey has occurred through the piece

sRK: Tutor's role is to evaluate the text and revision needed. (19)

Student 8: okay what else can I do, are the examples good or do you think I should change them?

ShRK: Session will culminate in pleasantries. (20)

Tutor 7: Excellent! Our time is up, but do you have any quick, last minute questions?

Student 8: not that I can think of right now. Thank you so much!

Tutor 7: No problem! Have a nice day/ =)

Student 8: you too!

Table 7.1. Tutors' 10 most frequent knowledge claims

Type of knowledge claim	Description	% of all tutor knowledge claims
tRK	Tutor's role is to suggest changes	11.0
tEK	Offer validation or affirmation	8.2
tRK	Tutor's role is to praise student	5.7
tRK	Tutor's role is to explain use of online tools	5.1
tWK	Genres have particular requirements or features	5.7
tRK	Tutor's role is to query student to set agenda	4.7
tRK	Student's role is to provide content knowledge	3.5
tRK	Tutor's role is to manage session time	3.3
tRK	Tutor's role is to read the text before commenting	3.1
tWK	Language correction	2.9

tRK = tutor role knowledge; tEK = tutor emotional knowledge; tWK = tutor writerly knowledge.

Table 7.2. Students' 10 most frequent knowledge claims

Type of knowledge claim	Description	% all student knowledge claims
sRK	Student's role is to be thankful	11.0
sRK	Tutor's role is to assess quality of student revision or proposed revision	8.7
sRK	Student's role is to give tutor affirmation	6.6
sRK	Student's role is to provide context for the writing	6.3
sRK	Tutor's role is to evaluate the text and revision needed	5.0
sEK	Express self-doubt or uncertainty	5.0
sWK	Areas of writerly attention include organization and argument/prompt	3.4
sRK	Tutor's role is to act as handbook	3.1
sEK	Offer context for error making	2.9
sEK	Express failure as a writer	2.9

sRK = student role knowledge; sEK = student emotional knowledge; sWK = student writerly knowledge.

A couple of observations on this "session": As someone who has conducted, observed, listened to, or read many hundreds of writing center sessions over the last thirty years, I am struck by its familiarity. This familiar nature reinforces, for me, the idea that writing center sessions are a distinct speech genre (Hymes 1989) with specific rules, roles, and responsibilities that each participant enacts, no matter the content of students' writing or the technology used (though, certainly, knowledge claims about how to use the online technology itself would not be present, in exactly that form, in face-to-face sessions, which involve other sorts of technologies). While that observation comes from a sense of familiarity, I am surprised by the relative lack of writerly knowledge talk in the data overall and as expressed in this manufactured session. And when this writerly talk occurs, primarily coming from tutors, it looks like the transmission model of education in which expert tutor knowledge is passed along to the novice student learner, rather than any real co-construction of knowledge.

Writing center curriculum, then as represented in this dataset, is much more about tutor-student rules, roles, and relationships than might be found in teacher-student interaction in a classroom. However, those roles put the tutor solidly in charge, directing actions on both participants' parts, including dispensing empathy to anxious students. In other words, based on this set of twenty online sessions, writing center curriculum is far less student-centered, far less co-constructed, and far more unidirectional than long-standing writing center theory and practice might lead one to believe.

TOWARD AN UNDERSTANDING OF WRITING CENTER CURRICULUM

My intent in this chapter was to offer a study of writing centers as curricular spaces, an accompaniment to their common portrayal as pedagogical spaces. What I found is that knowledge assertions or assertions of curriculum occupy a significant amount of time and space in my dataset of online writing center tutorials. The results of this study also offer empirical evidence to support or challenge common beliefs in writing center practice, specifically that sessions should be primarily focused on writers, not necessarily their writing; that nondirective tutoring is preferred to directive tutoring; and that the session should focus on higher-order concerns versus later-order concerns, each of which I take up in this discussion.

Writers versus writing: Stephen North's 1984 maxim has dominated a good deal of writing center theory and practice (see Boquet and Lerner

2015): "In a writing center the object is to make sure that writers, and not necessarily their texts, are what get changed by instruction. In axiom form it goes like this: Our job is to produce better writers, not better writing" (484). A common cautionary view of online tutorials is that they would, indeed, focus on the "writing," given its central role in a session, whether uploaded to the WCOnline space or sent via email in asynchronous tutoring. However, in this study, the great majority of knowledge claims did not necessarily focus on the writing. Instead, they focused on the writer and the tutor, particularly tutor and student assertions of each other's role. While North's maxim wouldn't quite have the rhetorical zing if it were rephrased as "Our job is to produce better tutors and writers or at least to (re)produce the conditions for tutors and writers to enact specific roles, not better writing," it would more accurately reflect what occurred in these twenty online sessions.

Directive versus nondirective tutoring: The debate about how "hands-on" or directive tutors should be is of long standing, with Brooks's (1991) "minimalist tutoring" often the preferred approach. As I have pointed out, none of the tutors in this study seemed to take a minimalist role; they usually positioned themselves and were positioned by students in directive roles. The curriculum here, particularly when it came to tutor and student assertions of role knowledge, meant that tutors dominated the online conversation.

Higher-order concerns versus later-order concerns: The common "we don't proofread" position of writing centers is meant to avoid the role of tutors as merely editors. Similarly, a common concern about online writing tutoring is that students' writing will be the center of attention in ways that might not happen in face-to-face sessions (Kastman Breuch 2005), and as a result, language-level editing will dominate. However, the sessions in this study had very little focus on language-level or later-order concerns, despite the wide variety of student writing projects and the several tutors and students involved. The curriculum was decidedly focused on higher-order concerns when it was not focused on tutor and student roles. Much more common for both tutors and students was to make knowledge claims about the particular features of the genres in which they were working.

While this study offers a starting point for understanding the curriculum of writing centers, several limitations are important to point out: twenty sessions over the course of one week are not necessarily representative of all sessions at this writing center, much less sessions at all writing centers. I also did not observe the specific preparation that these tutors had for their online work, preparation that might have strongly influenced the ways they interacted. Also, I did not seek true inter-rater reliability of the coding, instead performing an "audit" of an initial pass through the data and collaborating closely with my graduate research assistant, who did the bulk of the actual coding. Finally, I do not account for the tutor-student interactions that were not coded or that did not fall under one of the three kinds of knowledge claims (though a look at the HyperResearch coding environment, shown in appendix D, offers evidence that the great majority of the interaction did fall under the coding categories). The WCOnline synchronous tutoring environment includes a window for students to upload their writing and any other documents, for example, the assignments, and both tutor and student can edit and comment on these texts. I did not examine these practices. These limitations speak to the presence of bias and the lack of generalizability of this study. Nevertheless, the results themselves speak to the clear presence of a curriculum in writing center interaction, to the regularized dialog with specific tutor and student roles, and to the dominance of the interaction itself, rather than a focus on students' writing. This research also speaks to several questions for follow-up studies:

- Does the context of online synchronous tutoring determine curriculum? Would knowledge assertions be different in a face-to-face context? Similarly coding transcripts of a sample of face-to-face sessions for curricular assertions and comparing those results to online tutorials could highlight the importance of context.

- Do students' particular writing tasks or genres determine curriculum? The twenty sessions in this study do not offer enough variation in the kinds of writing students were doing to allow for analysis by task. A follow-up, then, over a much larger dataset would be to see the influence on the writing task itself, if any, on tutor and student knowledge claims.

- Do tutors have particular patterns of curricular claims? Of the fifteen tutors in this study, four worked with two different students over the course of the week, but no more than that. These small numbers do not offer much promise to investigate patterns of curricular claims for individual tutors (or students), but a larger dataset might offer insight into regularized ways in which tutors and students interact, as well as what might disrupt those regularized patterns.

Certainly writing centers will continue to be known as pedagogical spaces, particularly if their "brand" of one-to-one instruction and student-centered learning is offered to the rest of the university as applicable to a wide variety of subjects and contexts. Nevertheless, their identity as curricular spaces requires attention. In Boquet's (1999) article that I cited at the start of this chapter, she laments the identity of writing centers as "our little secret," little known to the rest of the campus community and to the wider field of writing studies. Articulations of curriculum might just be one way to let others in on that secret.

More broadly, the research I present in this chapter speaks to the ways that curriculum and pedagogy are always intertwined, that curriculum is always present in pedagogical contexts for learning and teaching writing, whether writing centers, writing classrooms, libraries, or coffee shops. What is essential is to recognize the distinct roles of each, particularly the ways that curriculum represents our values and is often expressed through our actions as much as through our syllabi, assignments sheets, and other curricular materials. In the next chapter, I describe possible directions for writing studies to acknowledge this central role of curriculum and build its design into everyday practices.

NOTES

1. For a similar claim about persistent marginalization in the context of Canadian higher education, see Paré 2017.
2. Northeastern University IRB Project #17-04-02.
3. I am indebted to Kyle Oddis, PhD student at Northeastern University at the time of this writing, for her hard work coding these transcripts.

8

THE FUTURE OF CURRICULUM IN WRITING STUDIES

On October 11, 2017, the Boy Scouts of America (BSA) announced that it would start accepting girls into its scouting ranks. While the BSA has seen no shortage of controversy, particularly because of the organization's grudging acceptance of gay scouts in its ranks and leadership positions, the decision to allow girls might be seen in its best light as an attempt at inclusivity and in its worst as a last-ditch effort to shore up rapidly falling ranks.

My interest, however, rests with curriculum and the values it embodies. In a *New York Times* article on this development, we learn that programming opportunities—that is, curriculum—differ between the two gendered scouting organizations. By allowing girls, the BSA was also giving girls curricular opportunities not usually available in the Girl Scouts. As one parent described, "If you have a daughter who's more rough and tumble, [Girl Scouts is] not going to be a good fit" (Bosman and Chokshi 2017).

Aside from the unfortunate stereotypes, I do wonder why, in the 105-year history of organized scouting in this country, the scouts themselves have not had a stronger role in shaping the curriculum of this organization. Or perhaps they have at the local level, but the national organization prefers to be the arbiter of curriculum, whether "rough and tumble" or more "domesticated." While the decline in the number of scouts is likely due to a whole host of factors, one central force could simply be scouts' opportunities, male or female, to have the agency to pursue the activities they feel most passionate about.

While scouting does not quite happen under the auspices of schooling, this situation nonetheless resembles schooling's reluctance to involve students in decisions about curriculum, particularly when it comes to the teaching of writing. In this chapter, I bring attention to several possibilities for a student role in curriculum design in writing classes in post-secondary education, efforts that are well aligned with writing studies' values for student-centered learning and student agency, values

DOI: 10.7330/9781607328810.c008

that have been expressed for a very long time at all levels of schooling. My intent is not to describe a specific curriculum, as I hope the project of this book shows the faults with a ready-made curriculum delivered from on high, no matter the intent to make it "student centered." Instead, I describe existing efforts to connect what happens in writing classrooms to students' "incomes" (Guerra 2008) or "funds of knowledge" (Esteban-Guitart and Moll 2014; Moje et al. 2004; Zipin 2009), efforts largely in the K–12 context but easily modified for post-secondary education. I also venture to Finland (well, virtually) to describe that country's efforts to involve students in curriculum construction. Finally, I point to ongoing research on what college seniors across three institutions describe as their "most meaningful" writing projects as a way to focus writing course curriculum and pedagogy on what students tell us they most value and why.

Overall, my emphasis in this final chapter is not on what a ready-made curriculum for writing studies might look like, but instead on how attention to the process of designing curriculum—and the necessity of including students in that process—has the potential to achieve goals for learning and teaching that writing studies has long proclaimed.

EVERYTHING OLD IS NEW AGAIN

Like most educational reforms, a focus on students as key partners in the creation of curriculum is not new. John Dewey, in *The Child and the Curriculum*, published in 1902, argues against the idea of expert-cultivated "subject-matter" transmitted to the naïve learner. Instead,

> the child is the starting-point, the center, and the end. His development, his growth, is the ideal. It alone furnishes the standard. To the growth of the child all studies are subservient; they are instruments valued as they serve the needs of growth. Personality, character, is more than subject-matter. Not knowledge or information, but self-realization, is the goal. To possess all the world of knowledge and lose one's own self is as awful a fate in education as in religion. Moreover, subject-matter never can be got into the child from without. Learning is active. It involves reaching out of the mind. It involves organic assimilation starting from within. Literally, we just take our stand with the child and our departure from him. It is he and not the subject-matter which determines both quality and quantity of learning. (9)

This student-centered approach to teaching was particularly meant to counter the division of subjects into specific disciplines in the belief that this organizational approach—reflected in distinct periods of time in the school day for mathematics, science, art, language, and so on—was not only unnatural in terms of how students best learn, but likely to result in bored and alienated students:

> If the subject-matter of the lessons be such as to have an appropriate place within the expanding consciousness of the child, if it grows out of his own past doings, thinkings, and sufferings, and grows into application in further achievements and receptivities, then no device or trick of method has to be resorted to in order to enlist "interest." The psychologized is of interest that is, it is placed in the whole of conscious life so that it shares the worth of that life. But the externally presented material, conceived and generated in standpoints and attitudes remote from the child, and developed in motives alien to him, has no such place of its own. Hence the recourse to adventitious leverage to push it in, to factitious drill to drive it in, to artificial bribe to lure it in. (27)

Dewey's emphasis on the connection between curriculum and students' "past doings, thinkings, and sufferings" leads easily to students having a central role in the creation of that curriculum, no matter the instructional level.

Zooming ahead some ninety-plus years, an often-cited source in higher education for new conceptions of learning and teaching is Robert Barr and John Tagg's (1995) "From Teaching to Learning: A New Paradigm for Undergraduate Education." In their article (cited in nearly 4,500 articles, according to Google Scholar), they assert that a shift to a "learning paradigm" has replaced the previous "instruction paradigm" in order to meet new challenges in colleges and universities. In the "learning paradigm," "a college's purpose is not to transfer knowledge but to create environments and experiences that bring students to discover and construct knowledge for themselves, to make students members of communities of learners that make discoveries and solve problems" (15). In this shift from teaching to learning, lectures are out, teaching as knowledge transmission or "banking" (Freire 1968) is out, coverage of material as primary goal is out, summative assessment alone is out. Despite the paradigmatic framing, Barr and Tagg don't believe that their student-centered approach would be difficult to implement: "The change that is required to address today's challenges is not vast or difficult or expensive. It is a small thing. But it is a small thing that changes everything. Simply ask, how would we do things differently if we put learning first? Then do it" (25). Some twenty or so years later, when I walk around my campus, I can unfortunately report that Barr and Tagg's paradigm shift is not quite fully shifted. The reasons for the entrenchment of instructional practices such as lecture and assessment as a measure of information recall are many, whether the resources needed, the emphasis on and rewards for faculty members' research over their teaching, the structure of curriculum and departments into disciplinary silos, or others. Still, my point here is that in education broadly the recognition of students and their learning as a starting point, rather than only an end goal, is of long standing.

In writing studies, putting students' experiences at the forefront is also of long standing, whether it's the Conference on College Composition and Communication's 1974 statement, "Students' Right to Their Own Language," attempts to focus first-year writing on students' "cultural rhetorics" (e.g., Kynard 2008; Stone and Stewart 2016), or endorsement of "translingual" approaches to teaching composition (Horner et al. 2011). A focus on student activity has also long been expressed in K–12 writing classrooms in terms of "problem-based" teaching (Applebee 1974, ch. 5). These efforts can be seen as part of a larger attempt to incorporate diversity and inclusion—creating opportunities for students historically marginalized from mainstream education to participate, learn, and succeed and to understand what students bring to the classroom as important "assets," rather than "deficits" to be corrected. Still, as I have pointed out throughout this book, these efforts are rarely marked as "curricular" and not seen as part of a cohesive attempt at curriculum design. For examples of those, I first turn to the K–12 realm, where visible attempts at curriculum change include "funds of knowledge" approaches, a focus on "authentic" writing tasks, and "culturally responsive teaching." I then point to efforts in higher education—whether specific to writing classes or more broadly—to include students in the process of curriculum design.

FROM A "DEFICIT-" TO AN "ASSET-BASED" APPROACH

The shift from a "deficit-" to an "asset-based" orientation to student learning has the strongest body of established literature in K–12 settings. One approach has been to investigate the "funds of knowledge" that students, particularly students of color and other nonmainstream populations, draw on in their literacy learning (see Esteban-Guitart and Moll 2014; Moje et al. 2004; Zipin 2009,). Moje and colleagues, in a study of the acquisition of scientific literacy by thirty middle school students in a predominantly Latinx, urban community of Detroit, found that "the youth we work with already draw upon many different funds, particularly outside of school. Their families, communities, peers, and popular culture all represent sources of knowledge about and ways of knowing the world, and many of these funds have direct connections to scientific literacy learning, as well as to literacy learning in other content areas"

(65). These connections, however, were not always utilized by students, leading Moje and her colleagues to conclude that "teachers and curriculum developers must develop deep understandings of the particular funds of knowledge and discourse that their students have available outside of school" (65).

In the building of curriculum, students' home and community or other out-of-school assets are essential to acknowledge and connect with. Esteban-Guitart and Moll (2014) add "identity" to the funds that are essential to successful learning and teaching: "Learning takes place when participants, supported and guided by others, are involved in activities that enact connections between prior knowledge and experiences (encrusted in their identities) and new information. In that regard, funds of identity acts as a lens through which we view and absorb new information and new identities. It is a dynamic composite of who we are and who we are becoming, based on what we have learned (and we are learning) from both our academic and everyday experiences" (44).

Another research strand aligned with a funds-of-knowledge approach draws attention to the need to create school-based "authentic literacy experiences," particularly for students of color and other nonmainstream groups. This conception calls for connecting what students write in school to "the real world" via "authentic" writing tasks (Behizadeh 2014, 28). Behizadeh argues that "authenticity" can be extended to students' school experiences, and that "to enact authentic writing instruction in schools, a need exists to investigate how students perceive authenticity in academic writing" (28). Based on interviews with twenty-two middle school students, Behizadeh found that authenticity was connected to students' having a choice to write about a topic they valued, to students' seeing their writing having an impact, and for students to express their points of view, rather than only to follow conventions (33). Muhammad and Behizadeh (2015), in an interview study of African American middle school students, similarly found that in addition to these qualities, students valued "writing that connects to students' lives and identities" (7).

These curricular approaches to connect students' learning to what they find meaningful are part of a larger movement toward "culturally responsive teaching" (Gay 2000). Gay writes that "the fundamental aim of culturally responsive pedagogy is to *empower* ethnically diverse students through academic success, cultural affiliation, and personal efficacy. Knowledge in the form of curriculum content is central to this empowerment. To be effective, this knowledge must be accessible to students and connected to their lives and experiences outside of school" (111). Gay's description of this approach echoes the notion that curriculum design needs to focus on "process and development" rather than as "product," as I argued in chapter 1: "If the 'creator, producer, and director' roles of students of color are circumscribed and they are seen only as 'consumers,' then the levels of their learning will also be restricted. This is too often true of present educational conditions. To reverse these trends, ethnically diverse students and their cultural heritages must be the sources and centers of educational programs" (111).

The goal of making students' lives and experiences "sources and centers of educational programs" is shared by all of these approaches toward "asset-based" pedagogy and curriculum. While in these research examples, the unit of instruction is usually the individual course or a set of linked courses, educational change—particularly when it comes to designing curriculum—also needs to occur at broader institutional levels, or perhaps be applied even more broadly. For an example of one such attempt, I turn to Finland and its educational system's development of "phenomenon-based" teaching.

PHENOMENON-BASED TEACHING IN FINLAND

Finland's educational system has had a long record of success when viewed through international measures of reading, math, and science achievement (Symeonidis and Schwarz 2016, 32). Further, according to former Finnish government official Pasi Sahlberg, the effort allowed individual schools to determine their curricula, following national values of "equity and equality": "During my time as a government school-improvement officer in the 1990s, I read hundreds of school-created curricula. All of the schools, with few exceptions, had formulated their values and goals with equity and equality as central principles of the declared work of the school" (2012, 28; see also Sahlberg 2015). Despite this focus and its record of educational success, the Finnish government in 2014 issued new guidelines for "basic education," reconceptualizing the shared and collaborative nature of curriculum development. Symeonidis and Schwarz (2016) cite the curriculum framework's justification for this approach: "The National Core Curriculum is based on the conception of learning that sees the pupils as active actors. They learn to set goals and to solve problems both independently and together with others. Learning is an inseparable part of an individual's growth as a human being and the building of a decent life for the community" (34).

Central to this approach is the requirement that each student will participate each year in at least one "multidisciplinary learning module," or ML, "studying what has been referred to as 'phenomena' or topics"

(Symeonidis and Schwarz 2016, 34): "MLs aim to engage students in exploring holistically authentic *phenomena*, which are interpreted as real-world themes and as such cannot be contained in only one subject. The purpose of MLs is to functionally approach and expand students' world of experience, strengthening their motivation and making learning meaningful to them" (35). The intent is that MLs are planned at the school level and are thus responsive to local needs and concerns. They are also intended to have students make connections between school, home, and their communities. As Symeonidis and Schwarz describe, "Key, however, in the design of MLs is the role of pupils, who actively take part in planning objectives, content and working methods" (35).

It is too early to draw conclusions from this effort, but I bring it up here as an example of how curriculum design, even at the national level, can be powered by a belief in students as the primary drivers of their learning, and that their lives, communities, and interests need to be the starting point of inquiry, just as Dewey pointed to in 1902.

LEARNING FROM AND WITH STUDENTS IN COLLEGE

Recently, as I waited my turn in the food line at a university teaching and learning center, where I had been invited to give a faculty workshop, I overheard one faculty member declare to a colleague, "Those international students come to us with such deficits." Such "deficit" attitudes toward student learning are stubbornly persistent in college-level writing, often reinforcing college writing as more about punishment for language transgressions than about inclusion of diverse abilities and experiences. While these attitudes are of long standing for a variety of ideological and historical reasons (Berlin 1987; Connors 1997; Crowley 1998), several lines of research in higher education take countering these attitudes as a starting point. One example comes from international research on "academic literacies." As Lillis and colleagues (2015) write, a "deep and consistent concern" for academic literacies researchers is with the limitations of much official discourse on language and literacy in a rapidly changing higher-education world. This included the prevailing deficit approach to language, literacy, and indeed students, whereby emphasis tends overwhelmingly to be on what student writers don't or can't do in academic writing rather than on what they can do (or would like to do), and where—even while discourses of diversity and internationalization populate university missions statements globally (5).

A research project that I have been involved in for the last several years is an attempt to resist this deficit orientation and to focus instead on how college seniors find their writing experiences to be meaningful (Eodice, Geller, and Lerner 2016). In surveys and interviews with seniors from three different institutions, we found that students cite as their most meaningful writing projects those that connected to their experiences, passions, and interests; to what they saw as relevant or connected to future paths; to those that offered opportunities for new experiences and exploring new content. Our follow-up survey and interviews with faculty whom students named as having taught the courses in which the meaningful writing projects occurred showed us that faculty often deliberately build these qualities into their curricula. While they were not necessarily co-constructing curriculum with students, they were creating opportunities for students to bring their assets and aspirations to their learning. In a sense, these assignments were framed "expansively" (Engle et al. 2012), offering students the spaces to bring what they valued in the past, present, or future to their writing.

Understanding the ways students find their writing experiences to be meaningful or might be repositioned as knowledge creators is well aligned with writing studies' values, whether those values are student agency or seeing the writing classroom as a site for knowledge transformation, rather than transmission of knowledge.[1] These efforts are also aligned with what Gere (2018, 139) reports in her study of University of Michigan undergraduates: students seek writerly agency not necessarily through the curricular paths we expect, whether that means pursuing a range of writing experiences in multiple disciplines (141) or investing their writing time in extracurricular activities (143).

What I am calling for here is to connect writing studies' familiar values for student learning to the process of curriculum design. Such an approach has the potential to overcome a legacy of writing classrooms as essentially unequal places. DeJoy (2004) points out this legacy in relation to first-year writing: "It would be impossible to change [writing studies] in any significant way without acknowledging and working to revise the unequal relationships that drive a situation in which literacy is, by definition, primarily an act of consumption and adaption for some and primarily an act of participation and contribution for others" (9). DeJoy calls instead for first-year writing classes to focus on "participation and contribution" rather than merely "consumption" of existing knowledge: "Participation and contribution are critical concepts in the learning processes that do not restrict teacher/learner relationships to consumption and reproduction. The idea that we come together to participate in and contribute to knowledge bases, pedagogies, value systems, and structures of learning is vital in first-year writing courses, where students are introduced to the expectations of composing (in) higher education, and where many faculty are introduced to the expectations they can/ should have for students and themselves as members of the composition community" (97).

It's also important to acknowledge the ways that institutions themselves limit these possibilities for students. Lillis's (2001) conclusion from her study of adult writers in UK higher education (or HE) is particularly cautionary: "It is difficult to get close to individual desires for meaning making within the context of culture of HE: student-writers' efforts are inevitably channeled into working out what is acceptable within HE, rather than exploring what they might want to mean" (162).

Still, examples abound of course- and institution-wide efforts to give students a role in shaping their futures. In many ways, recent efforts to foster undergraduate research, identified as a "high-impact practice" that increases students' engagement with their learning (Kuh 2008), can be seen as a way to involve students more fully in the design of curriculum (Grobman and Kinkead 2010; see also Fitzgerald 2013). As Grobman and Kinkead write, "Undergraduate research involves students as apprentices, collaborators, or independent scholars in critical investigations using fieldwork and discipline-specific methodologies under the sponsorship of faculty mentors. Students engaged in genuine research gain an insider's understanding of field-specific debates, develop relevant skills and insights for future careers and graduate study, and most important, contribute their voices to creating knowledge through the research process" (ix). This knowledge creation does not necessarily have to happen under the auspices of a class and is, instead, a way for students to make the curriculum their own, pursuing interests and questions that are meaningful.

Another manifestation of this asset-based approach to higher education is found in Kells's (2018) refocusing of writing across the curriculum as "writing across communities," with particular attention to language difference and bringing to the forefront students as "transcultural citizens." Kells offers essential questions to consider when being attentive to students' key role in curriculum design: "What are the characteristics of the discourse communities (personal, civic, and academic) that our students bring to university? How diverse are these practices and how does that diversity affect curricula?" (4). Ultimately, "a WACommunities approach to college writing instruction invites students to consider how an understanding of the dimensions of cultural diversity enhances their ability to write and communicate *appropriately* (i.e., with an awareness of different conventions), *productively* (i.e., so as to achieve their desired aims), *ethically* (i.e., to remain attuned to the communities they serve), *critically* (i.e., to learn to engage in inquiry and discovery), and *responsively* (i.e., to negotiate the tensions caused by the exercise of authority in their spheres of belonging)" (4–5).

In a broad approach to including students in the design of curriculum, Alison Cook-Sather, Peter Felten, and Catherine Bovill (Bovill, Cook-Sather, and Felten 2011; Cook-Sather, Bovill, and Felten 2014; see also Cecchinato and Foschi 2017) argue for the importance of creating "partnerships" between faculty and undergraduates:

> We define student-faculty partnerships as a collaborative, reciprocal process through which all participants have the opportunity to contribute equally, although not necessarily in the same way, to curricular or pedagogical conceptualization, decision making, implementation, investigation, or analysis. This definition stands in contrast to the student-as-consumer model that has become increasingly prevalent in higher education. It also departs from the traditional "sage-on-the-stage" model of teaching. Partnership, as we define it, positions both students and faculty as learners as well as teachers; it brings different but comparably valuable forms of expertise to bear on the educational process. In this way, partnership redefines the roles of student and faculty not only in relation to one another but also in relation to the institutions within which we work. Partnership redefines processes and therefore our approach to analysis, pedagogical practice, and research in ways that emphasize affirmation as well as create opportunities for change. (Cook-Sather, Bovill, and Felten 2014, 6–7)

Their book *Engaging Students as Partners in Learning and Teaching: A Guide for Faculty* offers extensive examples of what this partnership might look from a wide variety of institutional contexts and disciplines. What's key is that the process of partnering involves negotiation, honoring what both students and faculty bring to the design of learning:

> According to our guiding principles and definition, partnership involves negotiation through which we listen to students but also articulate our own expertise, perspectives, and commitments. It includes making collaborative and transparent decisions about changing our practices in some instances and not in others and developing mutual respect for the individual and shared rationales behind those choices. Indeed, it means changing our practices when appropriate, but also reaffirming, with the benefit of students' differently informed perspectives, what is already working well. Sometimes it means following where students lead, perhaps to places we may not have imagined or been to before. In all of these cases, respect and reciprocity are integral to the learning process: we share our perspectives and commitments and listen openly to students' insights, they share theirs and listen to ours, and in the exchange, we all become wiser. (8–9)

Cook-Sather, Bovill, and Felten (2014) point out that these partnerships can be on the classroom level, whether that's working with students to negotiate assessment criteria (see Inoue 2005) or involving undergraduate writing fellows to work with faculty on assignment design and implementation and to support students with their writing (Zawacki 2008). What's key here is that the process of partnership is dynamic, fluid, and ongoing, informed by past partnerships but also responsive to new partners—students and faculty—with new needs and new goals.

REVISITING SITES OF INQUIRY

The sites of inquiry I have explored in these chapters offer a variety of lessons when it comes to developing curriculum in writing studies:

- Curriculum design needs to be focused on "process and development."
- Curriculum needs to involve all stakeholders: students, faculty—including part-timers and adjuncts—and administrators.
- Curriculum needs to have a relationship to students' extracurriculum when possible.
- Curriculum design needs to acknowledge its relationship to pedagogy and pedagogical design.
- Curriculum design needs to acknowledge that curriculum is always present, whether or not we call it such.
- Curriculum design needs to reflect the values we hold dear—a belief in the importance of student agency, of honoring the assets they bring to instructional contexts, and of literacy's transformative potential.

As I described at the start of this book, the thoughtful and visible development of curriculum in writing studies is also necessary for the field to meet its disciplinary ambitions. That does not mean that the production of curriculum guides and mandated curricula necessarily needs to follow (though one might argue that such structures have long existed in the form of textbooks, particularly for first-year writing classes; see Miles 2000). Instead, we can rely on what we know about writing and student writers to set forth principles upon which curriculum might be constructed. One example of what that might look like is to start with a developmental model of learning rather than rely on a defined and fixed set of outcomes. For example, Beaufort's (2004) writing development model of five knowledge domains—rhetorical knowledge, writing process knowledge, genre knowledge, subject matter knowledge, and discourse community knowledge—offers a research-based framework for designing curriculum. While I would augment these knowledge domains with additions of students' development of knowledge as writers, as students, and as would-be professionals (see Lerner and Poe 2014), a curriculum could be created from this framework with tasks appropriate to varying levels of development and indexed to local context, student "incomes," and faculty expertise.

I also need to note that partnering with students to co-create curriculum and relying on students' many discursive and cultural assets does not mean being limited to the familiar or avoiding challenge. I am aligned with Miller (2015), who describes his approach to "slow reading" in his class and the importance of writing "at the edge of one's understanding" (162). One instructive finding from our research on students' meaningful writing projects (Eodice, Geller, and Lerner 2016) seems particularly relevant here: nearly eight in ten students reported that they had not written anything similar to what they described as their most meaningful writing project. Instead, opportunities to "to write at the edge of one's understanding" represented new challenges, new opportunities to learn, new possibilities for agency.

What is key is that curriculum is an expression of values, and as I have argued in this book, writing studies has a long history of making value propositions, whether those have to do with the importance of honoring what students bring to our classrooms and to our writing centers, of establishing reciprocal relationships with communities, or of advocating for inclusive practices and policies. Expressing those values in the form of curriculum is an essential next step, a way to ensure that the next wave of educational reform is more than mere fad but instead a thoughtful and comprehensive approach that focuses on student writers and their essential role in the design of their educational futures.

NOTE

1.   While a full treatment of the topic is a bit outside the bounds of this book, recent efforts to understand the ways students "transfer" their learning to and from writing courses (e.g., Donahue 2012; Driscoll and Wells 2012; Nowacek 2011; Reiff and Bawarshi 2011; Wardle 2009) have the potential to shed light on effective processes of curriculum construction, particularly if the focus is on students' experiences with curriculum, as is true in Nowacek's research.

APPENDIX A

SYLLABUS: FIRST-YEAR WRITING COURSE
FIRST-YEAR WRITING: ENGW1111

NEAL LERNER

COURSE DESCRIPTION

FROM THE COURSE CATALOG: First-Year Writing offers students the opportunity to study and practice writing in a workshop setting. Students read a range of texts in order to describe and evaluate the choices writers make and apply that knowledge to their own writing; learn to conduct research using primary and secondary sources; explore how writing functions in a range of academic, professional, and public contexts; and write for various purposes and audiences in multiple genres and media. Throughout the course, students give and receive feedback, revise their work, and reflect on their growth as writers.

SPECIFIC TO THIS SECTION: Students in this section of First-Year Writing will engage in a semester-long service learning (S-L) project, working with writers in a particular site of practice: high school students at the Edward M. Kennedy Academy for Health Careers (EMK), located in Cahners Hall on Northeastern's campus. I will ask you to sign up for **two hours of tutoring per week**, starting late Jan./early Feb. and going through the end of the semester, and joining us will be an S-L TA, who will help coordinate and support your S-L work. I will be providing more details on this project; for now, think of the Writers' Room as a place to practice what you are learning about **writing, literacy, and education**, as well as a kind of writing laboratory—a site for you to study writing in a context devoted to its practice and improvement.

Another manifestation of our class theme of **writing, literacy, and education** will be in the research and writing you do over the semester, whether exploring your own literacy experiences, making sense of the literacy experiences of your classmates, writing opinion pieces on issues specific to our theme, or conducting empirical research on your tutoring practices at the EMK. These activities are guided by the Writing Program Learning Goals (see below), the theme of this course, and the

DOI: 10.7330/9781607328810.c009

evolving needs of the class members. In other words, you can expect some degree of change as we proceed!

In addition to the two physical workspaces in which we will do our work together—the Northeastern University classroom and the EMK—we will also participate in two online workspaces: Blackboard and Digication. Blackboard will function as both a digital repository for course documents and a blogging space, where you will reflect on and write about the readings, conversations, and experiences of this course. You should already be enrolled by the registrar's office in the Blackboard version of this course. Make sure to check the Blackboard site on a regular basis for updates and announcements. You can also email me or your classmates from the Blackboard interface. Digication is an electronic portfolio (eportfolio) tool where a dynamic version of this syllabus will be found. You will also compose your final course eportfolio in Digication. I will introduce Digication to you early in the course, and you can decide whether and how to use it in advance of the final eportfolio.

CLASSROOM CLIMATE

This course is concerned with educational issues, which are inherently political and potentially divisive. Given the current political climate, many of us have strong feelings about both the tone and the result of the recent presidential election and about the policies and practices that will be rolling out in the coming months and years. At the same time—indeed, for this reason—this class will be a space devoted to free inquiry and an open exchange of ideas and perspectives. I expect everyone to help shape an inclusive learning environment that promotes regular productive participation by all members and is free of all forms of discrimination or harassment. This kind of learning environment features open discussion; collective confrontation of difficult questions and controversial ideas; and respect for cultural, linguistic, and intellectual diversity. While it is sometimes appropriate to share our beliefs and opinions, our goal in this course is to *inform* those beliefs and opinions through careful and organized inquiry and evidence-based thinking, research, and writing. I will evaluate your performance not on the content of your beliefs and opinions, but exclusively on the grading criteria set forth in this syllabus.

COURSE STRUCTURE

Our course will function as a seminar. In a seminar, lectures, if any, are infrequent.

You must come to each class prepared to discuss and write on the day's reading. You should plan to read the required reading twice before class discussion (and respond to it outside of class if required). Work closely with each text, identifying specific passages that are difficult, obscure, provocative, insightful. Mark these and record questions and comments that come to mind. Bring your notes and text to class always.

Preparation of written assignments entails rough drafts and exercises in revision and peer review. Before beginning a draft, you'll complete brief preliminary exercises to launch your inquiry. You'll write and submit a rough draft, which builds on these preliminary exercises. You'll then confer with fellow students in peer review; you are expected to read each other's work carefully and assess it in specific ways. With specific responses from your readers in mind and your own strategic thinking, you'll revise your rough draft into something polished and powerful.

All writing should be carefully proofread. Grammar and punctuation will be addressed as an integral part of the writing process. If you have special concerns with grammar and punctuation, please seek personal help from me and consultants at the writing center.

Please feel free to talk to me about any difficulties or concerns you may have. And let me know what you think is going well. Remember, your teachers are here to help, and I welcome any and all contact with you.

BOOKS AND OTHER MATERIALS TO PURCHASE

Rose, Mike. *Lives on the Boundary* (Penguin, 1989). Available at Northeastern Bookstore.

Additional readings available as pdfs on course Blackboard site.

Please always bring to class a working writing utensil and method for composition (pen and pencil, computer, iPad, etc.).

RECOMMENDED READING

A handbook of grammar, usage, and referencing format is highly recommended. Fortunately, several websites offer such handbooks free of charge. One of the most comprehensive is the Purdue Online Writing Lab (OWL): http://owl.english.purdue.edu/owl/.

PROJECT DESCRIPTIONS

ENGAGED CLASSROOM AND WRITERS' ROOM PARTICIPATION (15%): This is a small writing course and our class time will be devoted mainly to discussion and activities.

Therefore, I expect everyone to contribute *regularly* and *productively*. Moreover, I expect everyone to help shape a learning environment that promotes this level and quality of participation by all members. This kind of learning environment features open discussion and inquiry, the confrontation of hard questions and controversial ideas, and respect for intellectual, linguistic, and cultural diversity. These expectations apply to your participation in the classroom and at the Kennedy Academy. I will be receiving feedback from the teachers at EMK on the level and quality of your participation in that space.

Besides regular productive contributions to class and the EMK, peer-review activity, while not graded separately, is especially important to your participation grade.

Because feedback is important to writers, and because reading and providing response to other writers can help us improve our own writing, failure to participate in a peer-review session will result in a final participation grade not higher than a C, and two missed peer-review sessions will result in an F for participation.

BLOG: Throughout the semester, you will contribute weekly to a blog on our Blackboard course site. The purpose of the blog is to provide you with a space where you can *make sense* of our readings, conversations, and experiences in this course—by reflecting on our work together and with others, working with the readings, commenting or extending classroom discussion, generating ideas for and drafts of projects, trying out ideas that strike you without warning, collecting intriguing "found texts," experimenting with various media, etc. Each week (that is, by class time on Friday), you will be responsible for writing **a minimum of 500 words per week**—in as many weekly entries as you wish—as well as posting **a brief comment on the blog of at least one of your colleagues** per week. Your cumulative grade for the blog will be based upon your thoughtful completion of this informal but substantive writing and weekly commenting; I won't grade individual entries or evaluate the writing for grammar, mechanics, organization, etc. Ruthanne or I will offer a writing prompt on occasion, but your blog should be a place where you feel free to try out ideas, take risks, and explore without worrying about polishing your prose, as you will in your formal writing for the course. I do expect that you will **address each of the course readings** in your blog, but you should go well beyond individual "reading responses" to include more expansive, connected thinking. I also advise at least occasional close work with course texts, especially ones you find difficult and/or unfamiliar. Though I won't respond to every one of your posts—I will comment occasionally—you should always feel free to ask me to respond to anything you've written on the blog. Finally, at least *five* of your blog entries for the semester must incorporate significant reflection on your experiences at the Kennedy Academy in the context of our course readings and/or discussions. This does not include a final reflective entry, for which I will provide a specific prompt.

PROJECT 1—GUIDED SELF-PLACEMENT ESSAY ANALYSIS AND REVISIT: The purpose of this assignment is to have you engage with what is a fairly typical academic writing task: make sense of a large body of data, discerning patterns and trends, and then put those patterns and trends in dialog with what published scholars have had to say on those topics. A couple of wrinkles, however, in what is typical: the data you're grappling with are your and your classmates' guided self-placement essays (GSPE)/their experiences as readers and writers. And, ultimately, you'll put your own GSPE/literacy narrative into conversation with the experiences of your classmates and several of the readings you've completed. I describe this project in more detail in a specific assignment sheet.

PROJECT 2—OP-ED ON A TOPIC OF YOUR CHOICE: For this assignment, you will be writing an op-ed, which is a persuasive/argumentative essay, generally for a public audience. You will be taking a stand on some aspect of our class's focus—education and literacy—or choosing a topic that's of interest to you. An op-ed is a brief argumentative essay that takes a clear stand on an issue, provides evidence to support that stand, and has the goal of persuading the reader that the writer's position is valuable and believable. There are many organizational strategies you could pursue to make your essay convincing, and we'll discuss those in class. However, one good strategy is to find an editorial you find particularly effective—not because it takes a position with which you agree, but because of the ways the writer has argued for that position. Overall, editorials are usually relatively brief: 750–1,000 words.

PROJECT 3—RESEARCH ON TUTORIAL INTERACTION: The goal of this assignment is for you to observe, report on, and analyze a writing center tutorial. The framework for your analysis should come from one of the two analytical schemes described in chapter 10 of the Longman Guide to Peer Tutoring,[1] from the SPEAKING[2] scheme or the analysis of feedback sequences—or Thompson's ideas of "instruction," "cognitive scaffolding," and "motivational scaffolding" as described in "Scaffolding in the Writing Center."[3]

STEP 1: The source for your data is one of your or one of your peer's tutoring conferences at the Kennedy Academy. If for some reason you do not have opportunity to capture one of your conferences, I can make arrangements to have you observe a writing center conference at the Northeastern Writing Center in Holmes Hall. Whichever you do, you'll need to obtain the permission of both consultant and student (verbal permission is fine for this task).

If you are observing someone else's conference, you will need to take careful notes and, ideally, record the session itself (you can borrow a digital recorder from me or use your smartphone or other device).

STEP 2: You will analyze the session you observed with one or two analytical schemes from chapter 10 in the Longman Guide: Del Hyme's SPEAKING scheme or the analysis of feedback sequences or using Thompson's ideas of "instruction," "cognitive scaffolding," and "motivational scaffolding" as described in "Scaffolding in the Writing Center." You are also welcome to come up with your own analytical scheme.

STEP 3: You will work with at least two classmates to collaborate on a formal write-up of your tutorial analyses, looking for similarities and differences among the data you each collected. Your final version should include an introduction in which you offer context for your analysis, some sense of the "big picture" and the "so what," for example, what might we learn about writing center work by engaging in such an analysis? Similarly, your write-up should include a conclusion pointing to the implications of your analysis. Was what you observed unique in some ways? Would what you found be true for other sessions?

FINAL REFLECTIVE EPORTFOLIO: For your final project, you will use Digication software to build an electronic portfolio that does two things: (1) makes a case for and demonstrates how well you met, if not exceeded, the Writing Program Learning Goals in ENGW1111; (2) identifies a consistent theme or thread in your research and writing this semester.

Your eportfolio will be framed by a reflective introduction of roughly 500–750 words in which you present your claims about yourself as a writer, reader, and thinker, and point your reader to evidence in support of these claims. Essentially, your argument in this introduction is how well you met the WP Learning Goals, and the evidence to support that argument will come from your work this term.

In terms of that supporting evidence, what you include in your eportfolio will depend on the overall claim you're trying to make. For example, if you wish to demonstrate improvement over time, or features of your writing process, you may wish to include your guided self-placement essay, drafts, writer's notes, revision plans, reflective memos, peer reviews, responses to readings, or other assignments, as well as comments on your writing from others, whether from peers or from your instructor. You may also include writing you've done for other classes or for nonschool purposes if it clearly supports a claim you're making.

As always, your purpose and audience will determine how you design your text. How can you frame and organize the materials and design the eportfolio interface to best communicate and demonstrate your strengths? Should you use visuals? Would it be helpful to write short blurbs for the individual projects? Do you want to attach links or paste text into the page itself? You will face many such decisions, and I encourage you to be creative in the design of your eportfolio. This is a multimodal platform, and you should take advantage of its affordances. You want to spark your readers'/viewers' interest in your work and entice them to read through it. The eportfolios will be evaluated for how well you support the claims you make in your reflective introduction; how effectively the design of the eportfolio shapes the reading/viewing experience; and the quality of the individual artifacts.

GRADING/ASSESSMENT

Components / % of Final Grade

Engaged participation in class and at the Kennedy Academy: 15%
Weekly blog post and response: 15%

Project 1: 20%
Project 2: 20%
Project 3: 20%
Final reflection/assessment: 10%

Final Grades

Final grades will be calculated on a 100-point scale according to the following:

A	93–100	C	73–76.9
A-	90–92.9	C-	70–72.9
B+	87–89.9	D+	67–69.9
B	83–86.9	D	63–66.9
B-	80–82.9	D-	60–62.9
C+	77–79.9	F	59.9 and below

ABOUT NEAL LERNER

I have been a faculty member in the English department at Northeastern since 2011. For my first two years, I held the administrative role of writing center director, then I spent a year as director of writing in the disciplines, which means I coordinated the Advanced Writing in the Disciplines (AWD) course and worked with faculty across the university on teaching writing-intensive (WI) courses, and since 2014, I have been writing program director. Previous to joining Northeastern, I spent nine years as a lecturer and administrator in MIT's Writing across the Curriculum Program, primarily working with classes and students in biology and biological engineering. Before MIT, I was a faculty member and writing programs coordinator at the Massachusetts College of Pharmacy & Health Sciences. My research interests are in the history, theory, and practice of teaching writing, whether in classrooms, writing centers, science laboratories, or other settings. My doctoral degree is in education/literacy studies, and I also have an MA in English/creative writing, a high school English teaching credential, and a BA in English.

NORTHEASTERN UNIVERSITY WRITING PROGRAM POLICIES
WRITING PROGRAM LEARNING GOALS

The Writing Program comprises first-year writing courses, advanced writing in the disciplines courses, and the writing center. The goals below apply to all three sites, but our expectations for how well and to what extent students will accomplish the goals vary in each. You can find the learning goals on the Writing Program website, (http://www.northeastern.edu/writing/student-learning-goals-writing-program/).

1. Students write both to learn and to communicate what they learn.
2. Students negotiate their own writing goals and audience expectations regarding conventions of genre, medium, and situation.
3. Students formulate and articulate a stance through and in their writing.
4. Students revise their writing using responses from others, including peers, consultants, and teachers.
5. Students generate and pursue lines of inquiry and search, collect, and select sources appropriate to their writing projects.
6. Students effectively use and appropriately cite sources in their writing.
7. Students explore and represent their experiences, perspectives, and ideas in conversation with others.
8. Students use multiple forms of evidence to support their claims, ideas, and arguments.

9.   Students practice critical reading strategies.

10.   Students provide revision-based response to their peers.

11.   Students reflect on their writing processes and self-assess as writers.

COLLECTION OF STUDENT WORK FOR PROGRAM ASSESSMENT

Your instructor may be asked to submit one or more samples of your writing to the Writing Program Assessment Committee for the purpose of program assessment. Student work is randomly selected and used solely for the purpose of program-level assessment. Looking at student writing from a programmatic perspective helps us improve our program. Student writing collected for this purpose is never circulated outside the Writing Program for any reason. While we cannot guarantee that all identifying information will be removed from all materials read by Writing Program evaluators, we report only aggregate data to those outside the program; no teachers or student are identified in these reports. If you have any questions or concerns about our program assessment, feel free to contact Professor Neal Lerner, Writing Program Director, at n.lerner@neu.edu.

EMAIL POLICY

All students in first-year writing classes must use their Northeastern email addresses in order to receive email from their instructors and to access Blackboard sites for their writing courses.

A student must receive a grade of C or better in order to pass all required writing courses in the Department of English (C is required for graduation). Any student earning a C- or lower will need to repeat the course in order to fulfill the writing requirement. The instructor makes the final decision with respect to any grade between A and C. Any portfolio receiving lower than a C must be reviewed and signed off on by a committee of three to six Writing Program instructors.

COURSE POLICIES

ATTENDANCE & LATENESS

Writing Program policy requires regular attendance at class meetings. Students are allowed three unexcused absences in classes that meet for three days a week; they are allowed two unexcused absences in classes that meet for two days. During the summer sessions, students are allowed two unexcused absences. Significant and/or frequent tardiness may be counted as unexcused absences at the instructor's discretion.

Students also have the right to a limited number of excused absences due to a religious observance, illness, death in the family, required participation in athletic events, or other serious and unavoidable life circumstances. Students are responsible for notifying instructors when they must miss class for any reason. Instructors are responsible for determining whether a student will be excused from the class.

Instructors are reminded that University Health and Counseling Services will not issue documentation of students' illnesses or injuries. Because writing classes are conducted workshop-style and focus on revision, a student who misses too many class meetings or falls too far behind in making up work, even with a legitimate excuse, is not earning credit for the same course as the rest of the class. In that case, the instructor may suggest, but not require, that the student withdraw from rather than fail the course.

ACADEMIC INTEGRITY

Northeastern University is committed to the principles of intellectual honesty and integrity: the NU Academic Honesty and Integrity Policy is found at http://www.northeastern.edu/osccr/academic-integrity -policy/.

The Office of Student Conduct and Conflict Resolution (OSSCR) website (http://www.northeastern.edu/osccr/) provides extensive information on student conduct, the disciplinary process, and the range of available sanctions. All members of the Northeastern community are expected to maintain complete honesty in all academic work, presenting only that which is their own work in tests and assignments. In English classes, this definition of plagiarism applies not only to borrowing whole documents, but also to borrowing parts of another's work without proper acknowledgment and proper paraphrasing or quotation. We will discuss effective and responsible use of sources throughout the semester.

NOTES

1.   Gillespie and Lerner 2008.
2.   See Hymes 1974.
3.   See Thompson 2009.

APPENDIX B

WCONLINE SYNCHRONOUS TUTORING ENVIRONMENT

Welcome to your online consultation! The consultation module has a chat area on the right side, a document collaboration space or whiteboard area in the middle, a toolbar that includes an option to draw, and (if turned on at your center) an option to use audio and video.

TEXT CHAT: The right side of the screen is a text-based chat area. Type in the box at the lower right to have a text conversation. The text can either show up for the other participant in your session as you are typing, or show up only once you press 'enter' or 'return' on your keyboard. Keep the checkbox for 'send real time chat updates' (at the top of the chat column) checked to allow the other participant to see text as you are typing, or uncheck 'send real time chat updates' if you would prefer to type a whole chat before allowing the other participant to see what you have typed. In either case, press 'enter' or 'return' to have your complete comment/question show up in the chat column.

WHITEBOARD: The bulk of the screen, where this text is currently located, is the document collaboration whiteboard. Here, you can import a document, paste a document, or type text. Changes made to text in this window are seen immediately by both individuals participating in the online consultation.

TOOLBAR: The toolbar is across the top of the screen, or divided on the top and bottom if you are using a phone. The icons on the left side allow you to work with a document's formatting, such as by making text bold. The icons on the right side (or at the bottom) include options for your online session, such as importing a document and drawing. Hover over any icon for a text label showing the icon's function.

- Import/Export: The icon showing two arrows allows you to upload a document to share with the other participant in this consultation. Both of you can type on the document. Once the consultation is over, you can choose to save the document on your computer using the same icon.

- Timeslider: After your consultation, use the clock icon to play back the text changes to the document, starting from the beginning of your session.

- Show the users on this pad: The icon with a person symbol and a number allows you to type a different name (such as a nickname) and/or choose a color to highlight your typing, as well as to see the name of the other participant in the session.

DRAWING FUNCTION: Using the pencil icon, open an area that allows you to draw on top of the document collaboration whiteboard. Within the drawing area, there are additional options to draw with a thick brush or thin pencil, change colors, clear your drawing, or use a solid white background. If you would like to draw without seeing the any text in the background, select the white square to make the drawing area no longer see-through. Diagrams, pictures, math problems, etc. are saved within your online session but do not appear in an exported document.

- Expanding and minimizing: On a computer, after you have clicked the pencil icon, hover over the drawing area to expand it, and hover away from it (such as over the chat area) to minimize it. On a touch screen, touch the pencil icon once to open the drawing function and a second time to expand the drawing area. A third touch closes the drawing area.

AUDIO AND VIDEO, IF ENABLED: With audio/video enabled for your center's online sessions, your browser will most likely ask if you would like to allow use of your camera and microphone in this session. The specific prompt depends on your browser, device, and operating system. Follow your browser's instructions to start using audio/video. If you deny access to the camera and microphone or close the question without making a selection, click on the video camera icon to reopen the option. If you are not prompted to allow your camera and microphone, close your online meeting in your current browser and open it in a different browser. Hover over your own image in the video to see options to mute the audio or hide the video.

AFTER YOUR SESSION: Your chat and document will be saved in this online meeting. You can always come back by viewing your appointment and clicking the 'start or join online consultation' link.

QUESTIONS: If you have any questions, click the question mark at the top right for more information.

DOI: 10.7330/9781607328810.c010

APPENDIX C

FREQUENCY OF STUDENT AND TUTOR KNOWLEDGE CLAIMS WITH EXAMPLES

ROLE KNOWLEDGE

Tutors' most frequent role knowledge claims

Description	Total	% this type	% all types
Tutor's role is to suggest changes. final paragraph should be the one that begins with "too often in healthcare"	54	17.4	11.0
Tutor's role is to praise student. Okay, you've got some really great ideas in here!	28	9.0	5.7
Tutor's role is to explain use of online tools. just paste the link in this chat box and make sure the share settings give anyone with the link access	25	8.1	5.1
Tutor's role is to query student to set agenda. Great, got it. Now what were you hoping to work on today?	23	7.4	4.7
Student's role is to provide content knowledge So I would include info about your family, and whatever else you think makes you stand out	17	5.5	3.5
Tutor's role is to manage session time. Do you want to take a 5 min. writing break and try to add some of your personal piece into what you have so far?	16	5.2	3.3
Tutor's role is to read the text before commenting. Awesome—give me just a moment to read	15	4.8	3.1
Student's role is to evaluate revisions or edits. I just changed "educational change" to "policy change" in the sentence that starts "The goal of this study" . . . do you think anything is lost in that change?	14	4.5	2.9
Tutors role is to check student's understanding. Well, what do you think the purpose of the conclusion is here?	14	4.5	2.9
Student's role is to offer verbal clarity. what do you mean?	13	4.2	2.7

continued on next page

DOI: 10.7330/9781607328810.c011

Tutors' most frequent role knowledge claims—*continued*

Description	Total	% this type	% all types
Tutor's role is to focus revision priorities. I think you're focusing on the right aspects, I'm just wondering what you would like to work on at the moment, since we have the outline and this first part.	13	4.2	2.7
Tutor's role is to offer evaluation of student's text. Okay, you've got some really great ideas in here! I think your argument for her autonomy is very strong, and you use some great quotes for evidence	12	3.9	2.4
Tutor's role is to attend to student's agenda. Okay having read over the letter from your professor, and knowing you wanted to look at structure, let's focus on your introduction first.	11	3.5	2.2
Tutor's role is to interpret instructor's intent. Did your professor say whether or not they had a preference to overall formatting of the quotes i.e. MLA or APA or Chicago, etc.?	11	3.5	2.2
Student's role is to provide context. the topic was this	10	3.2	2.0
Student's role is to set the agenda. Hello! I was wondering if you could help me with the organization of thoughts in this essay, or let me know if my argument follows correctly	8	2.6	1.6
Tutor needs permission from student to review text. I'm going to take a few minutes to read this over, okay?	6	1.9	1.2
Student's role is to revise. Notice on others you only capitalize the first word of the title.	5	1.6	1.0
Tutor's role is to clarify terms. so, I think this argument is good, but it is a lot of the same argument in each paragraph	5	1.6	1.0
Tutor's role is to seek student feedback on session's effectiveness. We are out of time for today, do you have any last questions?	4	1.3	0.8
Tutors should defer to student's expertise about particular genres. you could say that later in the chapter, I think (and you probably do!)	3	1.0	0.6
Tutor's role is not to correct for grammar. so, we don't correct for grammar but I am happy to ask questions as I read through	2	0.6	0.4
Tutor's role is to provide resources. For details of what APA needs in the bibliography have a look at the Purdue OWL website which describes citation methods	1	0.3	0.2

continued on next page

Students' most frequent role knowledge claims—*continued*

Description	Total	% this type	% all types
Student's role is to be thankful. ok thanks for sharing. I think we are at our 45 mins. you were helpful	42	17.1	11.0
Tutor's role is to assess quality of student revision or proposed revision. Do you think for what I learned from being a stage manager is attractive enough?	33	13.4	8.7
Student's role is to give tutor affirmation. Got it.	25	10.2	6.6
Student's role is to provide context for the writing. I have a paper to work on. The requirement of the first part is shown on the left	24	9.8	6.3
Tutor's role is to evaluate the text and revision needed. what parts in the paper you think are relatively less important?	19	7.7	5.0
Tutor's role is to act as handbook. is it right to use present tense when you talk about things happened in the story?	12	4.9	3.1
Tutor's role is to clarify. grandparents don't count, correct?	10	4.1	2.6
Student's role is to evaluate the text. it's worth 15% of my grade and I think it could be much better	9	3.7	2.4
Tutor's role is to help. okay, what do you think I should do to make the [text] better?	9	3.7	2.4
Tutor's role is to instruct on use of online tools. I can email the rough draft to me how do I get it on the board	9	3.7	2.4
Student's role is to revise. that's it excellent. I can do that.	8	3.3	2.1
Student's role is to set the agenda. i also uploaded the grading criteria for this paper, can you please read that one?	7	2.8	1.8
Tutor's role is to offer genre knowledge. Mainly looking for an effective personal statement	7	2.8	1.8
Student's role is to interpret instructor's intent. he said she hated the whole "five paragraph essay" format and said it should be more of our view on things, our take on things, including our voice and all so i've been struggling to grasp what that means, but I feel like I finally do kinda get that, so now I'm just worried about the whole organization, if things sound alright, aspect of things	6	2.4	1.6
Student's role is to offer text for feedback. Here's the intro to my chapter 3.	6	2.4	1.6
Student's role is to revise in response to tutor's comments. okay i agree, i can do that!	5	2.0	1.3

continued on next page

Students' most frequent role knowledge claims—*continued*

Description	Total	% this type	% all types
Student's role is to revise—and soon! i think that's it! thank you for your help, i'll work on those changes now!	5	2.0	1.3
Professor's concerns are a driving force for revision. I don't know. But she marks it in the same spot each time. I don't know if I just need to add the doi or if it's a punctuation error, or something else . . .	4	1.6	1.0
Student's role is to revise—but not immediately. just cause i wanna make sure when i work on it again I don't lose track of what I'm doing	4	1.6	1.0
Tutor can also set agenda. I have a rough draft of an education narrative due and I also have to annotate a peer review research article. Do you have a preference?	2	0.8	0.5

Tutor's most frequent writerly knowledge claims

Description	Total	% this type	% all types
Genres have particular requirements or features. and then in a bibliography at the end you would list all texts, giving details like author, place of publication and date	28	23.5	5.7
Need for clear flow of ideas. I think if you connected more to the Anatomy of Dependence, and less on the linguistic relativity, it would be a good starting point.	18	15.1	3.7
Need for clarity. Oh, okay. I do think rewording it would help there—I think the idea is getting lost, and it's a really interesting point.	17	14.3	3.5
Language correction. That was just a matter of a run-on sentence, I think.	14	11.8	2.9
Need for concision. That first one was just that the sentence had a lot going on, and I though it might be served better by breaking up the ideas into seperate sentences.	9	7.6	1.8
Each paragraph should have a clear focus. For the second paragraph, I think it might be better to focus your ideas a bit before you continue writing.	8	6.7	1.6
First paragraphs offer a focus/goal. Your very first paragraph, which is the introduction, we see simply you. Your reader is not introduced to the website, why they may be interested, or what you will continue to discuss throughout your paper. You spend a long time getting into your subject matter and thus lose space to go in depth on the website, it's language and uses.	6	5.0	1.2
Conclusions restate main ideas. the job of the conclusion is to summarize your major points in the essay and tell the reader why your ideas are important	5	4.2	1.0

continued on next page

Tutor's most frequent writerly knowledge claims—*continued*

Description	Total	% this type	% all types
Assignment prompts should be addressed. It should be something that directly answers the question in the prompt	4	3.4	0.8
Thesis should be supported with evidence. you reiterate your main point in each para, but not as much time is spent showing how each additional example deepens or changes your original argument	4	3.4	0.8
Need for clear first sentences. I think having that topic sentence to make it clear what question is being answered will make it clear that things that may sound similar aren't redundant, that they're answering different questions.	3	2.5	0.6
Punctuation or capitalization correction. yes your use of the semi-colon is spot on i fixed your mistake where your capitalizing certain words	3	2.5	0.6

Students' most frequent writerly knowledge claims

Description	Total	% this type	% all types
Areas of writerly attention include organization and argument/ prompt. I was wondering if you could help me with the organization of thoughts in this essay, or let me know if my argument follows correctly.	13	20.3	3.4
Instructor's directions are a driving and complicating force. so my teacher was like "you can make your project into an art piece, or a video, be risky if you hate essays!" and i said no.	8	12.5	2.1
Genres have particular features. it just should show my research background and educational / work but it should be formal	6	9.4	1.6
Need for revision. might be too shallow? repetitive? . . . what i know is that i can put more examples in it to better illustrate	6	9.4	1.6
Essays should be coherent. what points or idea you think is too shallow in the paper? what points does't make sense(because I'm not sure if i express it in an easy understand way)	5	7.8	1.3
Punctuation or capitalization needs attention. Is it the punctuation?	4	6.3	1.0
Citations need to be formatted correctly. I don't know if I just need to add the doi or if it's a punctuation error, or something else	3	4.7	0.8
Conclusions should be conclusive. yeah I don't know what to say/if the conclusion is okay	3	4.7	0.8

continued on next page

Students' most frequent writerly knowledge claims—*continued*

Description	Total	% this type	% all types
Essays need arguments. Can you check like do arguments make sense and easy to understand?	3	4.7	0.8
Essays should be focused. I think I will focus on my professional experience	3	4.7	0.8
Introductions might have problems. I want to start my personal statement with something less cliche than I am applying for this program because / . . .	3	4.7	0.8
Papers should be finished. I am not finished yet with the paper	2	3.1	0.5
Paragraphs need topic sentences. I don't know if I am fully answering the questions if my examples are even relevant to the topic and of the paragraph	2	3.1	0.5
Potentially unclear meaning is a cause for concern. I have to make sure I put it in. I don't know if i did.	2	3.1	0.5
Paragraphs need concluding sentences. should I also give a concluding sentence to each paragraph?	1	1.6	0.3

Tutors' most frequent emotional knowledge claims

Description	Total	% this type	% all types
Offer validation or affirmation. Hi, no worries at all!	40	66.7	8.2
Express empathy for student error or effort. no need to worry! we can figure it out over this session	11	18.3	2.2
Express interest or enthusiasm. Okay, this sounds like an interesting essay! Give me a little while to read it through	10	16.7	2.0

Students' most frequent emotional knowledge claims

Description	Total	% this type	% all types
Express self-doubt or uncertainty. i understand what you're saying, but i'm not entirely sure i know how to go about doing that	19	26.8	5.0
Offer context for error making. English is not my first language and I just want to make sure the ideas are good and that it allows + makes sense	13	18.3	3.4
Express failure as a writer. I'm not good at grammers. it has been a pain in the ass for my writing	11	15.5	2.9

continued on next page

Students' most frequent emotional knowledge claims—*continued*

Description	Total	% this type	% all types
Express interest or enthusiasm. Okay, good!	11	15.5	2.9
Express confidence. I think the logic of the paper is pretty solid.	9	12.7	2.4
Express unfamiliarity with platform or tools. is there a way to do voice chat with this? that would allow me to multitask a bit better.	8	11.3	2.1

APPENDIX D

EXAMPLE OF HYPERRESEARCH CODING ENVIRONMENT

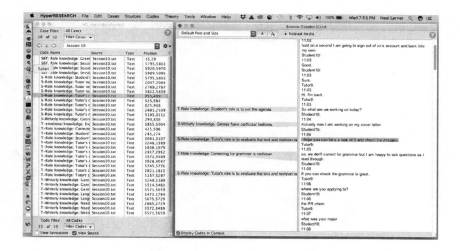

DOI: 10.7330/9781607328810.c012

REFERENCES

Abell, Sandra K. 2008. "Twenty Years Later: Does Pedagogical Content Knowledge Remain a Useful Idea?" *International Journal of Science Education* 30 (10): 1405–16.

Adler-Kassner, Linda. 2012. "The Companies We Keep; or, The Companies We Would Like to Try to Keep: Strategies and Tactics in Challenging Times." *Writing Program Administration* 36 (1): 119–40.

Adler-Kassner, Linda, and Elizabeth Wardle, eds. 2015. *Naming What We Know: Threshold Concepts of Writing Studies.* Logan: Utah State University Press.

Adler-Kassner, Linda, and Elizabeth Wardle, eds. 2016. *Naming What We Know: Threshold Concepts of Writing Studies, Classroom Edition.* Logan: Utah State University Press.

Akbar, Amna. 2013. "How Tarek Mehanna Went to Prison for a Thought Crime." *Nation,* December 31.

Alexander, Jonathan, and Jacqueline Rhodes. 2012. "Flattening Effects: Composition's Multicultural Imperative and the Problem of Narrative Coherence." *College Composition and Communication* 65 (3): 430–54.

Andersen, Travis. 2014. "US Court Won't Hear Appeal by Terror Plotter Mehanna." *Boston Globe,* October 6.

Annual Report of the Board of Education and Superintendent of City Schools with Rules and Regulations of the City Schools of Los Angeles, CA, 1897–98. 1898. Los Angeles: Board of Education.

Anyon, Jean. 1980. "Social Class and the Hidden Curriculum of Work." *Journal of Education* 162 (1): 67–92.

Applebee, Arthur N. 1974. *Tradition and Reform in the Teaching of English: A History.* Urbana, IL: NCTE.

Applebee, Arthur N., and Judith A. Langer. 2011. "A Snapshot of Writing Instruction in Middle Schools and High Schools." *English Journal* 100 (6): 14–27.

Aronson, Brittany, and Judson Laughter. 2016. "The Theory and Practice of Culturally Relevant Education: A Synthesis of Research across Content Areas." *Review of Educational Research* 86 (1): 163–206.

Arum, Richard, and Josipa Roksa. 2010. *Academically Adrift: Limited Learning on College Campuses.* Chicago: University of Chicago Press.

Ayers, William, Therese Quinn, David Stovall, and Libby Scheiern. 2008. "Teachers' Experience of Curriculum: Policy, Pedagogy, and Situation." In *The SAGE Handbook of Curriculum and Instruction,* edited by F. Michael Connelly, 306–26. Los Angeles: SAGE.

Barr, Robert, and John T. Tagg. 1995. "From Teaching to Learning: A New Paradigm for Undergraduate Education." *Change* 27:12–25.

Bazerman, Charles, Arthur N. Applebee, Virginia W. Berninger, Deborah Brandt, Steve Graham, Paul Kei Matsuda, Sandra Murphy, Deborah Wells Rowe, and Mary Schleppegrell. 2017. "Taking the Long View on Writing Development." *Research in the Teaching of English* 51 (3): 351–60.

Beaufort, Anne. 2004. "Developmental Gains of a History Major: A Case for Building a Theory of Disciplinary Writing Expertise." *Research in the Teaching of English* 39 (2): 136–85.

Beaufort, Anne. 2012. "The Matters of Key Knowledge Domains and Transfer of Learning in the Outcomes Statement." *Writing Program Administration* 36 (1): 180–87.

Behizadeh, Nadia. 2014. "Adolescent Perspectives on Authentic Writing Instruction." *Journal of Language & Literacy Education* 10 (1): 27–44.

DOI: 10.7330/9781607328810.c013

Behm, Nicholas N., Gregory R. Glau, Deborah H. Holdstein, Duane Roen, and Edward M. White. 2013a. Introduction to *The WPA Outcomes Statement—A Decade Later*, edited by Nicholas N. Behm, Gregory R. Glau, Deborah H. Holdstein, Duane Roen, and Edward M. White, ix–xvii. Anderson, SC: Parlor.

Behm, Nicholas N., Gregory R. Glau, Deborah H., Holdstein, Duane Roen, and Edward M. White, eds. 2013b. *The WPA Outcomes Statement—A Decade Later*. Anderson, SC: Parlor.

Benda, Jon, Michael Dedek, Kristi Girdharry, Chris Gallagher, Neal Lerner, and Matthew Noonan. 2018. "Confronting 'Superdiversity' in US Writing Programs." In *The Internationalization of US Writing Programs*, edited by Shirley K Rose and Irwin Weiser, 79–96. Logan, UT: Utah State University Press.

Bennett, William. 1996. *The Book of Virtues*. New York: Simon & Schuster.

Berlin, James A. 1987. *Rhetoric and Reality: Writing Instruction in American Colleges, 1900–1985*. Urbana: Southern Illinois University Press.

Black, Paul. 2000. "Formative Assessment and Curriculum Consequences." In *Curriculum and Assessment*, edited by David Scott, 7–23. Westport, CT: Greenwood.

Black, Rebecca W. 2009. "Online Fan Fiction, Global Identities, and Imagination." *Research in the Teaching of English* 43 (4): 397–425.

Boquet, Elizabeth H. 1999. "'Our Little Secret': A History of Writing Centers, Pre– to Post–Open Admissions." *College Composition and Communication* 50 (3): 463–82.

Boquet, Elizabeth H., and Neal Lerner. 2008. "After 'The Idea of a Writing Center.'" *College English* 71 (2): 170–89.

Bosman, Julie, and Niraj Chokshi. 2017. "Boy Scouts Will Accept Girls, in Bid to 'Shape the Next Generation of Leaders.'" *New York Times*, October 11. https://www.nytimes.com/2017/10/11/us/boy-scouts-girls.html.

Bovill, Catherine, Alison Cook-Sather, and Peter Felten. 2011. "Students as Co-creators of Teaching Approaches, Course Design, and Curricula: Implications for Academic Developers." *International Journal for Academic Development* 16 (2): 133–45.

Brands, H. W. 1995. *The Reckless Decade: America in the 1890s*. Chicago: University of Chicago Press.

Brodkey, Linda. 1994. "Making a Federal Case out of Difference: The Politics of Pedagogy, Publicity, and Postponement." In *Writing Theory and Critical Theory*, edited by John Clifford and John Schilb, 236–61. New York: MLA.

Brooks, Jeff. 1991. "Minimalist Tutoring: Making the Student Do All the Work." *Writing Lab Newsletter* 15 (6): 1–4.

Brooks, Kevin. 2002. "Composition's Abolitionist Debate: A Tool for Change." *Composition Studies* 30 (2): 27–41.

Burstall, Sara A. 1909. *Impressions of American Education in 1908*. New York: Longmans, Green.

Canagarajah, A. Suresh. 2006. "The Place of World Englishes in Composition: Pluralization Continued." *College Composition and Communication* 57 (4): 586–619.

Carillo, Ellen C. 2017. "The Evolving Relationship between Composition and Cognitive Studies: Gaining Some Perspective on Our Contemporary Moment." In *Contemporary Perspectives on Cognition and Writing*, edited by Patricia Portanova, J. Michael Rifenburg, and Duane Roen, 39–55. Boulder: WAC Clearinghouse and University Press of Colorado.

Cazden, Courtney B. 2001. *Classroom Discourse: The Language of Teaching and Learning*. 2nd ed. Portsmouth, NH: Heinemann.

Cecchinato, Graziano, and Laura Carlotta Foschi. 2017. "Flipping the Roles: Analysis of a University Course Where Students Become Co-creators of Curricula." *Teaching and Learning Together in Higher Education* 22. http://repository.brynmawr.edu/tlthe/vol1/iss22/5.

Champlin, Dell P., and Janet T. Knoedler. 2016. "Commodification of Labor, Teaching, and Higher Education." Paper presented at the Annual Meeting of the Association for Evolutionary Economics, Portland, OR, January 3.

"Cleveland Shooter Had Military Training." 2003. CBSNEWS.com, May 11.

Commonwealth of Massachusetts, Executive Office of Labor and Workforce Development. 2012. "Labor Market Information, 2012." http://www.mass.gov/lwd/economic-data/.

Conference on College Composition and Communication. 1974. "Students' Right to Their Own Language." *College Composition and Communication* 25 (3): 1–32.

Connors, Robert J. 1997. *Composition-Rhetoric: Backgrounds, Theory, and Pedagogy.* Pittsburgh: University of Pittsburgh Press.

Cook-Sather Alison, Catherine Bovill, and Peter Felten. 2014. *Engaging Students as Partners in Learning and Teaching: A Guide for Faculty.* San Francisco: Jossey-Bass.

Council of Writing Program Administrators. 2014. "WPA Outcomes Statement for First-Year Composition (v3.0)." http://wpacouncil.org/positions/outcomes.html.

Council of Writing Program Administrators, National Council of Teachers of English, and the National Writing Project. 2011. *Framework for Success in Postsecondary Writing.* http://wpacouncil.org/files/framework-for-success-postsecondary-writing.pdf.

Crowley, Sharon. 1998. *Composition in the University: Historical and Polemical Essays.* Pittsburgh: University of Pittsburgh Press.

Davis, Kevin. 1995. "Life outside the Boundary: History and Direction in the Writing Center." *Writing Lab Newsletter* 20 (2): 5–7.

Davis, Matthew, and Kathleen Yancey. 2014. "Notes toward the Role of Materiality in Composing, Reviewing, and Assessing Multimodal Texts." *Multimodality and Assessment.* Special Issue, *Computers & Composition* 31: 13–28.

Davis, Roger P., and Jerry L. Hoffman. 2008. "Higher Education and the P-16 Movement: What Is to Be Done?" *Thought & Action* (Fall): 123–34.

Dedek, Michael. 2016. "Practicing Change: Curricular Innovation and Change in Writing Programs." PhD diss., Northeastern University.

DeJoy, Nancy C. 2004. *Process This: Undergraduate Writing in Composition Studies.* Logan: Utah State University Press.

Dewey, John. 1902. *The Child and the Curriculum.* Chicago: University of Chicago Press.

Dewey, John. 1915. *The School and Society.* Chicago: University of Chicago Press.

Donahue, Christiane K. 2012. "Transfer, Portability, Generalization: (How) Does Composition Expertise 'Carry'?" In *Exploring Composition Studies: Research, Scholarship, and Inquiry for the Twenty-First Century,* edited by Kelly Ritter and Paul Matsuda, 145–66. Logan: Utah State University Press.

Downs, Doug. 2010. "Writing-about-Writing Curricula: Origins, Theories and Initial Field-Tests, No. 12." *WPA-CompPile Research Bibliographies.* http://comppile.org/wpa/bibliographies/Bib12/Downs.pdf.

Downs, Doug, and Liane Robertson. 2015. "Threshold Concepts in First-Year Composition." In *Naming What We Know: Threshold Concepts of Writing Studies,* edited by Linda Adler-Kassner and Elizabeth Wardle, 105–21. Logan: Utah State University Press.

Downs, Doug, and Elizabeth Wardle. 2007. "Teaching about Writing, Righting Misconceptions: (Re)Envisioning 'First-Year Composition' as 'Introduction to Writing Studies.'" *College Composition and Communication* 58 (4): 552–71.

Downs, Doug, and Elizabeth Wardle. 2012. "Reimagining the Nature of FYC: Trends in Writing-about-Writing Pedagogies." In *Exploring Composition studies,* edited by Kelly Ritter and Paul Kei Matsuda, 123–44. Logan: Utah State University Press.

Driscoll, Dana, and Sherry Lynn Perdue. 2012. "Theory, Lore and More: An Analysis of RAD Research in the *Writing Center Journal,* 1980–2009." *Writing Center Journal* 32 (1): 11–39.

Driscoll, Dana Lynn, and Jennifer Holcomb Marie Wells. 2012. "Beyond Knowledge and Skills: Writing Transfer and the Role of Student Dispositions in and beyond the Writing Classroom." *Composition Forum* 26. http://compositionforum.com/issue/26/beyond-knowledge-skills.php.

Ede, Lisa. 1989. "Writing as a Social Process: A Theoretical Foundation for Writing Centers?" *Writing Center Journal* 9 (2): 3–13.

"Educational Ideas: P. W. Search Delivers an Interesting Address." 1894. *Los Angeles Times*, September 18, 3.

Elbow, Peter. 2005. "A Friendly Challenge to Push the Outcomes Statement Further." In *The Outcomes Book: Debate and Consensus after the WPA Outcomes Statement*, edited by Susanmarie Harrington, Keith Rhodes, Ruth Overman Fischer, and Rita Malenczyk, 177–90. Logan: Utah State University Press.

Engle, Randi A., Diane P. Lam, Xenia S. Meyer, and Sarah E. Nix. 2012. "How Does Expansive Framing Promote Transfer? Several Proposed Explanations and a Research Agenda for Investigating Them." *Educational Psychologist* 47 (3): 215–31.

Eodice, Michele, Anne Ellen Geller, and Neal Lerner. 2016. *The Meaningful Writing Project: Writing, Teaching, and Learning in Higher Education.* Logan: Utah State University Press.

Epstein, Pam. 2000. "1896: The American Protective Association." http://projects.vassar.edu/1896/apa.html.

Ericsson, Patricia Freitag. 2005. "Celebrating through Interrogation: Considering the Outcomes Statement through Theoretical Lenses." In *The Outcomes Book: Debate and Consensus After the WPA Outcomes Statement*, edited by Susanmarie Harrington, Keith Rhodes, Ruth Overman Fischer, and Rita Malenczyk, 104–17. Logan: Utah State University Press.

Esteban-Guitart, Moisés, and Luis C. Moll. 2014. "Funds of Identity: A New Concept Based on the Funds of Knowledge Approach." *Cultural & Psychology* 20 (1): 31–48.

Fitzgerald, Lauren. 2013. "Undergraduate Writing Tutors as Researchers: Redrawing Boundaries." *Writing Center Journal* 33 (2): 17–35.

Freire, Paolo. 1968. *Pedagogy of the Oppressed.* New York: Seabury.

Gallagher, Chris W. 2012. "The Trouble with Outcomes: Pragmatic Inquiry and Educational Aims." *College English* 75 (1): 42–60.

Gay, Geneva. 2000. *Culturally Responsive Teaching: Theory, Research, & Practice.* New York: Teachers College Press.

Gee, James Paul. 2007. *What Video Games Have to Teach Us about Learning and Literacy.* 2nd ed. London: Palgrave Macmillan.

Gere, Anne Ruggles. 1994. "Kitchen Tables and Rented Rooms: The Extracurriculum of Composition." *College Composition and Communication* 45 (1): 75–92.

Gere, Anne Ruggles. 2018. "The Ways Our Students Write Now." *PMLA* 133 (1): 139–45.

Gillespie, Paula, and Neal Lerner. 2008. *The Longman Guide to Peer Tutoring,* 2nd ed. Boston: Longman.

Giroux, Henry A. 1988. *Teachers as Intellectuals: Toward a Critical Pedagogy of Learning.* Santa Barbara, CA: Praeger.

Giroux, Henry A., and David E. Purpel. 1983. *The Hidden Curriculum and Moral Education: Deception or Discovery?* Berkeley, CA: McCutchab.

Green, Constance McLaughlin. 1939. *Holyoke, Massachusetts: A Case History of the Industrial Revolution in America.* New Haven: Yale University Press.

Greene, Thomas C. 2003. "Hacking Victim Goes Postal." *Register*, May 12. https://www.theregister.co.uk/2003/05/12/hacking_victim_goes_postal/.

Grimm, Nancy M. 1996. "The Regulatory Role of the Writing Center: Coming to Terms with a Loss of Innocence." *Writing Center Journal* 17 (1): 5–29.

Grimm, Nancy M. 2011. "Retheorizing Writing Center Work to Transform a System of Advantage Based on Race." In *Writing Centers and the New Racism*, edited by Laura Greenfield and Karen Rowan, 75–100. Logan: Utah State University Press.

Grobman, Laurie, and Joyce Kinkead. 2010. "Introduction: Illuminating Undergraduate Research in English." In *Undergraduate Research in English Studies*, edited by Laurie Grobman and Joyce Kinkead, ix–xxxii. Urbana, IL: NCTE.

Guerra, Juan C. 2008. "Cultivating Transcultural Citizenship: A Writing across Communities Model." *Language Arts* 85 (4): 296–304.

Hairston, Maxine. 1992. "Diversity, Ideology, and Teaching Writing." *College Composition and Communication* 43: 179–95.

Hansen, Kristine. 2012. "The *Framework for Success in Postsecondary Writing*: Better Than the Competition, Still Not All We Need." *College English* 74 (6): 540–43.

"Hard Knocks: Prof. P. W. Search has a Few Words to Say." 1895. *Los Angeles Times,* June 23, 12.

Harrington, Susanmarie. 2005. "Introduction: Celebrating and Complicating the Outcomes Statement." In *The Outcomes Book: Debate and Consensus After the WPA Outcomes Statement,* edited by Susanmarie Harrington, Keith Rhodes, Ruth Overman Fischer, and Rita Malenczyk, xv–xix. Logan: Utah State University Press.

Harrington, Susanmarie, Keith Rhodes, Ruth Overman Fischer, and Rita Malenczyk, eds. 2005. *The Outcomes Book: Debate and Consensus After the WPA Outcomes Statement.* Logan: Utah State University Press.

Harris, Muriel. 1995. "Talking in the Middle: Why Writers Need Writing Tutors." *College English* 57 (1): 27–42.

Hartford, William F. 1990. *Working People of Holyoke: Class and Ethnicity in a Massachusetts Mill Town, 1850–1960.* New Brunswick: Rutgers University Press.

Haswell, Richard H. 2005a. "NCTE/CCCC's Recent War on Scholarship." *Written Communication* 22 (2): 198–223.

Haswell, Richard H. 2005b. "Outcomes and the Developing Learner." In *The Outcomes Book: Debate and Consensus after the WPA Outcomes Statement,* edited by Susanmarie Harrington, Keith Rhodes, Ruth Overman Fischer, and Rita Malenczyk, 191–200. Logan: Utah State University Press.

Heath, Shirley Brice. 1984. *Ways with Words: Language, Life and Work in Communities and Classrooms.* Cambridge: Cambridge University Press.

Heilker, Paul, and Peter Vandenberg, eds. 1996. *Keywords in Composition Studies.* Portsmouth, NH: Heinemann.

Hesse, Douglas D. 2005. "CCCC Chair's Address: Who Owns Writing?" *College Composition and Communication* 57 (2): 335–56.

Hiaasen, Scott. 2002. "Death Penalty Sought in CWRU Siege." *Cleveland Plain Dealer,* May 30.

Hiaasen, Scott, and John Mangels. 2003. "Loner's Rage Burned After Ruin of Web Site." *Cleveland Plain Dealer,* May 11.

Hirsch, E. D., Jr. 1987. *Cultural Literacy: What Every American Needs to Know.* New York: Random House.

Hobson, Eric H. 1997. "Ensuring Safety in the Writing Center." *Writing Lab Newsletter* 21 (10): 4–7.

Hokanson, Robert O'Brien. 2005. "Using Writing Outcomes to Enhance Teaching and Learning: Alverno College's Experience." In *The Outcomes Book: Debate and Consensus After the WPA Outcomes Statement,* edited by Susanmarie Harrington, Keith Rhodes, Ruth Overman Fischer, and Rita Malenczyk, 150–60. Logan: Utah State University Press.

"Holyoke, Mass." 1899. *School and Home Education* 18 (5): 264.

Holyoke School Committee. 1897. "Annual Report of the School Committee for 1897: Superintendent's Report." 207–64.

"Holyoke's Schools: Board Will Sustain New Superintendent in Contemplated Reforms." 1896. *Boston Daily Globe,* July 22, 7.

Horner, Bruce, Min-Zhan Lu, Jacqueline Jones Royster, and John Trimbur. 2011. "Language Difference in Writing: Toward a Translingual Approach." *College English* 73 (3): 303–21.

"How They Stand: Members of the Board of Education talk." 1985. *Los Angeles Times,* June 19, 8.

Hymes, Dell H. 1974. *Foundations of Sociolinguistics: An Ethnographic Approach.* Philadelphia: University of Pennsylvania Press.

Hymes, Dell H. 1989. "Ways of Speaking." In *Explorations in the Ethnography of Speaking,* 2nd ed., edited by Richard Bauman and Joel Sherzer, 433–51. Cambridge: Cambridge University Press.

Ingersoll, Richard, Lisa Merrill, and Daniel Stuckey. 2014. *Seven Trends: The Transformation of the Teaching Force*, updated April 2014. CPRE Report (#RR-80). Philadelphia: Consortium for Policy Research in Education, University of Pennsylvania.

Inoue, Asao B. 2005. "Community-Based Assessment Pedagogy." *Assessing Writing* 9:208–38.

"It Is Done: The School Board Has Ousted Superintendent Search." 1895. *Los Angeles Times*, June 21, 6.

Kastman Breuch, Lee-Anne. 2005. "The Idea(s) of an Online Writing Center: In Search of a Conceptual Model." *Writing Center Journal* 25 (2): 21–38.

Kells, Michelle Hall. 2018. "Writing across Communities." In *The TESOL Encyclopedia of English Language Teaching*, edited by John I. Liontas, 1–7. New York: John Wiley & Sons.

Kelly, A. V. 2004. *The Curriculum: Theory and Practice*. 5th ed. London: Sage.

Kesegich, Ken. 2003. "May 9, 2003." *CWRU Magazine* (Summer): 4–5.

Kidder, Tracy. 1989. *Among schoolchildren*. New York: Avon.

Kinloch, Valerie Felita. 2005. "Revisiting the Promise of *Students' Right to Their Own Language*: Pedagogical Strategies." *College Composition and Communication* 57 (1): 83–113.

Kinloch, Valerie, Tanja Burkhard, and Carlotta Penn. 2017. "When School Is Not Enough: Understanding the Lives and Literacies of Black Youth." *Research in the Teaching of English* 52 (1): 34–54.

Kleickmann, Thilo, Steffen Tröbst, Aiso Heinze, Andrea Bernholt, Roland Rink, and Mareike Kunter. 2017. "Teacher Knowledge Experiment: Conditions of the Development of Pedagogical Content Knowledge." In *Competence Assessment in Education: Research, Models and Instruments*, edited by Detlev Leutner, Jens Fleischer, Juliane Grünkorn, and Eckhard Klieme, 111–29. Cham, Switzerland: Springer.

Kuh, George D. 2008. *High-Impact Educational Practices: What They Are, Who Has Access to Them, and Why They Matter*. Washington, DC: American Academy of Colleges & Universities. http://www.neasc.org/downloads/aacu_high_impact_2008_final.pdf.

Kynard, Carmen. 2008. "'The Blues Playingest Dog You Ever Heard Of': (Re)Positioning Literacy through African American Blues Rhetoric." *Reading Research Quarterly* 43 (4): 356–73.

Lerner, Neal. 1996. "The Institutionalization of Required English." *Composition Studies* 24 (1–2): 44–60.

Lerner, Neal. 2000. "Confessions of a First-Time Writing Center Director." *Writing Center Journal* 21 (1): 29–48.

Lerner, Neal. 2009. *The Idea of a Writing Laboratory*. Carbondale: Southern Illinois University Press.

Lerner, Neal. 2014. "Writing Center Pedagogy." In *Guide to Composition Pedagogies*, 2nd ed., edited by Gary Tate, Kurt Schick, Amy Rupiper Taggart, and Brooke Hessler, 301–16. New York: Oxford University Press.

Lerner, Neal, and Mya Poe. 2014. "Writing and Becoming a Scientist: A Longitudinal Qualitative Study of Three Science Undergraduates." In *Applied Linguistics and Literacies for STEM: Founding Concepts, Methodologies and Research Projects*, edited by Mary Jane Curry and David I. Hanauer, 43–63. Amsterdam: John Benjamins.

Lewis, Edwin Herbert. 1897. *First Book in Writing English*. London: MacMillan.

Lillis, Theresa. 2001. *Student Writing: Access, Regulation, Desire*. London: Routledge.

Lillis, Theresa, Kathy Harrington, Mary Lea, and Sally Mitchell. 2015. Introduction to *Working with Academic Literacies: Case Studies toward Transformative Practice*, edited by Theresa Lillis, Kathy Harrington, Mary Lea, and Sally Mitchell, 3–22. Ft. Collins, CO: WAC Clearinghouse/Parlor.

"The Little Red Schoolhouse: Attitude of the American Protective Association." 1895. *Los Angeles Times*, May 8, 6.

Loucks, Michael K. 2009. "Sudbury Man Charged with Conspiracy to Provide Material Support to Terrorists." October 21. http://www.usdoj.gov/usao/ma.

Lu, Min-Zhan. 1998. "From Silence to Words: Writing as Struggle." In *Women/ Writing/ Teaching*, edited by Jan Zlotnik Schmidt, 133–48. New York: SUNY Press.

Ludy, Benjamin T. 2006. *A Brief History of Modern Psychology*. Hoboken, NJ: Wiley-Blackwell.

Lunsford, Andrea. 1991. "Collaboration, Control, and the Idea of a Writing Center." *Writing Center Journal* 12 (1): 3–10.

Luthra, Sahil. 2012. "Alex Morse '11: 100 Days as Mayor of Holyoke." *Brown Daily Herald*, April 11. http://www.browndailyherald.com/alex-morse-11-100-days-as-mayor-of -holyoke-1.2727858#.

Malenczyk, Rita, Susan Miller-Cochran, Elizabeth Wardle, and Kathleen Blake Yancey. 2018. *Composition, Rhetoric, & Disciplinarity*. Logan: Utah State University Press.

March, Andrew F. 2012. "A Dangerous Mind?" *New York Times*, April 21, SR1.

Massachusetts Department of Elementary and Secondary Education. 2011a. "Cohort 2010 Four-Year Graduation Rates—State Results." http://www.doe.mass.edu/infoservices /reports/gradrates/10_4yr.pdf.

Massachusetts Department of Elementary and Secondary Education. 2011b. "School District Profiles, 2011." http://profiles.doe.mass.edu/state_report/gradrates.aspx.

Matsuda, Paul Kei. 2003. "Process and Post-Process: A Discursive History." *Journal of Second Language Writing* 12: 65–83.

McComiskey, Bruce. 2012. "Bridging the Divide: The (Puzzling) *Framework* and the Transition from K–12 College Writing Instruction." *College English* 74 (6): 537–40.

McKinney, Jackie Grutsch. 2005. "Leaving Home Sweet Home: Towards Critical Readings of Writing Center Spaces." *Writing Center Journal* 25 (2): 6–20.

McMillan, Laurie. 2011. "Review of Wardle, Elizabeth, and Doug Downs, *Writing about Writing: A College Reader*." *Composition Forum* 24. http://compositionforum.com/issue/24 /writing-about-writing-review.php.

McSheffrey, Donald J. 1968. "Seek to Get Bigger, Better College in City; Still Fight New Outbreaks of Disastrous Fire." *Holyoke Daily Transcript*, January 5. http://holyokemass .com/quickclicks/qc_002_hsfire/index.html.

Mickelson, John M. 1972. "Personalized Instruction: How New Is It?" *Education Digest* 38 (3): 38–40.

Miles, Libby. 2000. "Constructing Composition: Reproduction and WPA Agency in Textbook Publishing." *WPA: Writing Program Administration* 24 (Fall/Winter): 29–53.

Miles, Libby, Michael Pennell, Kim Hensley Owens, Jeremiah Dyehouse, Helen O'Grady, Nedra Reynolds, Robert Schwegler, and Linda Shamoon. 2008. "Commenting on Douglas Downs and Elizabeth Wardle's 'Teaching about Writing, Righting Misconceptions.'" *College Composition and Communication* 59 (3): 503–11.

Miller, Carolyn. 1984. "Genre as Social Action." *Quarterly Journal of Speech* 70 (2): 151–67.

Miller, Richard E. 2005. *Writing at the End of the World*. Pittsburgh: University of Pittsburgh Press.

Miller, Richard E. 2015. "On Digital Reading." *Pedagogy: Critical Approaches to Teaching Literature, Language, Composition, and Culture* 16 (1): 153–64.

Moje, Elizabeth Birr, Kathryn McIntosh Ciechanowski, Katherine Kramer, Lindsay Ellis, Rosario Carrillo, and Tehani Collazo. 2004. "Working toward Third Space in Content Area Literacy: An Examination of Everyday Funds of Knowledge and Discourse." *Reading Research Quarterly* 39 (1): 38–71.

"Mr. Search Resigns: The Superintendent of School Will Retire at End of Term." 1898. *Holyoke Daily Transcript*, November 12, 1.

Muhammad, Gholnecsar E., and Nadia Behizadeh. 2015. "Authentic for Whom? An Interview Study of Desired Writing Practices for African American Adolescent Learners." *Middle Grades Review* 1 (2): article 5.

Murphy, Shelley. 2010. "Taking Refuge Where His Woes Began: Sudbury Terror Suspect Presses Case on Internet." *Boston Globe*, February 11, A1, A5.

Meyer, Jan H. F., and Ray Land. 2003. "Threshold Concepts and Troublesome Knowledge: Linkages to Ways of Thinking and Practising within the Disciplines." In *Improving Student Learning: Ten Years On*, edited by Chris Rust, 412–24. Oxford: Oxford Centre for Staff and Learning Development.

National Center for Higher Education Management Systems. NCHEMS Information Center for Higher Education Policy Making and Analysis. 2008. "College Participation Rates: College-Going Rates for High School Graduates—Directly from High School." http://www.higheredinfo.org/dbrowser/?year=2008&level=nation&mode=data&state =0&submeasure=63.

National Educational Association. 1894. *Report of the Committee of Ten on Secondary School Studies*. New York: American Book.

National Research Council. 2000. *How People Learn: Brain, Mind, Experience, and School*. Washington, DC: National Academy Press.

Newkirk, Thomas. 1989. "The First Five Minutes: Setting the Agenda in the Writing Conference." In *Writing and Response: Theory, Practice, and Research*, edited by Chris M. Anson, 317–31. Urbana, IL: NCTE.

Nichols, Jim. 2005. "Shooting Defendant Ruled Competent." *Cleveland Plain Dealer*, April 20.

Nieto, Sonia, Patty Bode, Eugenie Kang and John Raible. 2008. "Identity, Community, and Diversity: Retheorizing Multicultural Curriculum for the Postmodern Era." In *The SAGE Handbook of Curriculum and Instruction*, edited by F. Michael Connelly, 176–97. Los Angeles: SAGE.

North, Stephen M. 1984. "The Idea of a Writing Center." *College English* 46 (5): 433–46.

Nowacek, Rebecca S. 2011. *Agents of Integration: Understanding Transfer as a Rhetorical Act*. Carbondale: Southern Illinois University Press.

Numrich, Carol. 1996. "On Becoming a Language Teacher: Insights from Diary Studies." *TESOL Quarterly* 30 (1): 131–53.

"Organization and Use of a Writing Laboratory: Report of Workshop No. 9." 1951. *College Composition* and *Communication* 2:17–18.

Paré, Anthony. 2017. "The Once and Future Writing Centre: A Reflection and Critique." *Canadian Journal for Studies in Discourse and Writing/RéDactologie* 27:1–8. http://journals .sfu.ca/cjsdw/index.php/cjsdw/article/view/573.

Powers, Martine. 2012. "Hard-Charging Start for Youngest Mass. Mayor." *Boston Globe*, July 24, A1. http://articles.boston.com/2012-07-24/metro/32804027_1_youngest -mayor-elaine-pluta-mayoral-race.

"Preston W. Search: Educator, Author, Traveler." n.d. UC Berkeley Music Library Archives, Preston Willis Search Collection.

"P. W. Search Succumbs to Stroke: Famed Carmel Educator Is Fatally Stricken at River-side." 1932. *Monterey Peninsula Herald*, December 13, 1, 5.

Rankins-Robertson, Sherry. 2013. "The Outcomes Statement as Support for Teacher Creativity: Applying the WPA OS to Develop Assignments." In *The WPA Outcomes Statement—A Decade Later*, edited by Nicholas N. Behm, Gregory R. Glau, Deborah H. Holdstein, Duane Roen, and Edward M. White, 58–70. Anderson, SC: Parlor.

Reiff, Mary Jo, and Anis Bawarshi. 2011. "Tracing Discursive Resources: How Students Use Prior Genre Knowledge to Negotiate New Writing Contexts in First-Year Composition." *Written Communication* 28:312–37.

Riley, Terrance. 1994. "The Unpromising Future of Writing Centers." *Writing Center Journal* 15 (1): 20–34.

Roozen, Kevin. 2010. "Tracing Trajectories of Practice: Repurposing in One Student's Developing Disciplinary Writing Processes." *Written Communication* 27 (3): 318–54.

Rose, Mike. 1985. "The Language of Exclusion: Writing Instruction at the University." *College English* 47 (4): 341–59.

Rudolph, Frederick. 1990. *The American College & University: A History*. Athens: University of Georgia Press.

Russell, David R. 1991. *Writing in the Academic Disciplines, 1870–1990: A Curricular History.* Carbondale: Southern Illinois University Press.

Sahlberg, Pasi. 2012. "Quality and Equity in Finnish Schools." *School Administrator* (September): 27–30.

Sahlberg, Pasi. 2015. *Finish Lessons, 2.0.* New York: Teachers College Press.

Salvatori, Mariolina Rizzi, ed. 1996. *Pedagogy: Disturbing History, 1819–1929.* Pittsburgh: University of Pittsburgh Press.

Schubert, William H. 2008. "Curriculum Inquiry." In *The SAGE Handbook of Curriculum and Instruction*, edited by F. Michael Connelly. 399–419. Los Angeles: SAGE.

Search, Preston W. 1892. "The Old and the New in Education." Address to Colorado State Teachers' Association Conference, December 29.

Search, Preston W. 1894. "Individual Teaching: The Pueblo Plan." *Educational Review* 7 (2): 154–70.

Search, Preston W. 1895. "Individualism in Mass Education." *Journal of Proceedings and Addresses, Session of the Year 1895, Held at Denver, Colorado.* 398–411. St. Paul, MN: National Educational Association.

Search, Preston W. 1895. "The Los Angeles Contest." *Advance in Education* 1 (1): 24–26.

Search, Preston W. 1896. *Annual Report of the School Committee for 1896: Inaugural Address: Outlines of an Ideal School System*, 2868–92. Holyoke, MA: Holyoke School Committee.

Search, Preston W. 1897. *Annual Report of the School Committee for 1897: Report XVIII: Superintendent's Report*, 207–64. Holyoke, MA: Holyoke School Committee.

Search, Preston W. 1898. "The Elimination of Waste." *School Journal* 57 (16): 421.

Search, Preston W. 1901. *An Ideal School.* New York: Appleton.

Segall, Avner. 2004. "Revisiting Pedagogical Content Knowledge: The Pedagogy of Content/The Content of Pedagogy." *Teaching and Teacher Education* 20: 489–504.

Severino, Carol. 2012. "The Problems of Articulation: Uncovering More of the Composition Curriculum." *College English* 74 (6): 533–36.

Shamoon, Linda K., and Deborah H. Burns. 1995. "A Critique of Pure Tutoring." *Writing Center Journal* 15 (2): 134–51.

Shor, Ira. 1986. *Culture Wars: School and Society in the Conservative Restoration, 1969–1984.* New York: Routledge & K. Paul.

Shor, Ira. 1987. *Critical Teaching and Everyday Life.* Chicago: University of Chicago Press.

Shor, Ira. 1996. *When Students Have Power: Negotiating Authority in a Critical Pedagogy.* Chicago: University of Chicago Press.

Shulman, Lee S. 1986. "Those Who Understand: Knowledge Growth in Teaching." *Educational Researcher* 15 (2): 4–14.

Smitherman, Geneva. 2003. "The Historical Struggle for Language Rights in CCCC." In *Language Diversity in the Classroom: From Intention to Practice*, edited by Geneva Smitherman and Victor Villanueva, 7–39. Carbondale: Southern Illinois University Press.

Snyder, Thomas D., ed. 1993. *120 Years of American Education: A Statistical Portrait.* Washington, DC: U.S. Department of Education, National Center for Education Statistics.

Spitz, Julia. 2011. "Who Is the Real Tarek Mehanna?" *Metrowest Daily News*, February 24.

Stone, Brian J., and Shawanda Stewart. 2016. "HBCUs and Writing Programs: Critical Hip Hop Language Pedagogy and First-Year Student Success." *Composition Studies* 44 (2): 183–86.

Sullivan, Patrick. 2012. "Essential Habits of Mind for College Readiness." *College English* 74 (6): 547–53.

Summerfield, Judith, and Philip M. Anderson. 2012. "A Framework Adrift." *College English* 74 (6): 544–47.

Symeonidis, Vasileios, and Johanna F. Schwarz. 2016. "Phenomenon-Based Teaching and Learning through the Pedagogical Lenses of Phenomenology: The Recent Curriculum Reform in Finland." *Forum Oświatowe* 28 (2): 31–47. http://forumoswiatowe.pl/index.php/czasopismo/article/view/458.

Tate, Gary, Amy Rupiper Taggert, Kurt Schick, and H. Brooke Hessler, eds. 2013. *The Guide to Composition Pedagogies.* 2nd ed. New York: Oxford University Press.

Taylor, J. S. 1902. "Search's 'Ideal School.'" *School Journal,* February 8, 166.

Thomas, Susan. 2013. "The WPA Outcomes Statement: The View from Australia." In *The WPA Outcomes Statement—A Decade Later,* edited by Nicholas N. Behm, Gregory R. Glau, Deborah H. Holdstein, Duane Roen, and Edward M. White, 165–78. Anderson, SC: Parlor.

Thompson, Isabelle. 2009. "Scaffolding in the Writing Center: A Microanalysis of an Experienced Tutor's Verbal and Nonverbal Tutoring Strategies." *Written Communication* 26 (4): 417–53.

Tyack, David, and William Tobin. 1994. "The 'Grammar' of Schooling: Why Has It Been So Hard to Change?" *American Educational Research Journal* 31 (3): 453–79.

United States District Court for the District of Massachusetts. 2009. Search and Seizure Warrant. Case No. 09-120-LTS.

U.S. Department of Commerce, United States Census Bureau. 2010. "State and County Quick Facts. Holyoke, Massachusetts." http://quickfacts.census.gov/qfd/states/25/25 30840.html.

Valencia, Milton J., and John R. Ellement. 2009. "Records Show Man Intent on Terror, But Supporters Skeptical." *Boston Globe* October 22, A10.

Villanueva, Victor. 1993. *Bootstraps: From an American Academic of Color.* Urbana, IL: NCTE.

Wardle, Elizabeth. 2008. "Continuing the Dialogue: Follow-up Comments on 'Writing, Righting Misconceptions.'" *College Composition and Communication* 60 (1): 175–81.

Wardle, Elizabeth. 2009. "'Mutt Genres' and the Goal of FYC: Can We Help Students Write the Genres of the University?" *College Composition and Communication* 60 (4): 765–89.

Wardle, Elizabeth, and Doug Downs. 2010. *Writing about Writing: A College Reader.* Boston: Bedford/St. Martin's.

Wardle, Elizabeth, and Doug Downs. 2013. "Reflecting Back and Looking Forward: Revisiting 'Teaching about Writing, Righting Misconceptions' Five Years on." *Composition Forum* 27. http://compositionforum.com/issue/27/reflecting-back.php.

Wardle, Elizabeth, and Doug Downs. 2014. *Writing about Writing: A College Reader.* 2nd ed. Boston: Bedford/St. Martin's.

Wardle, Elizabeth, and Doug Downs. 2016. *Writing about Writing: A College Reader.* 3rd ed. Boston: Bedford/St. Martin's.

Washburne, Carleton W. 1918. "Breaking the Lock Step in Our Schools." *School and Society* 8 (197): 391–402.

Williams, William. 1892. *Composition and Rhetoric by Practice.* Boston: D. C. Heath.

Yancey, Kathleen Blake. 2001. "A Brief Introduction: WPA Outcomes Statement for First-Year Composition." *College English* 63 (3): 321–25.

Yancey, Kathleen Blake. 2004. "Made Not Only in Words: Composition in a New Key." *College Composition and Communication* 56 (2): 297–328.

Yancey, Kathleen Blake. 2005. "Standards, Outcomes, and All That Jazz." In *The Outcomes Book: Debate and Consensus After the WPA Outcomes Statement,* edited by Susanmarie Harrington, Keith Rhodes, Ruth Overman Fischer, and Rita Malenczyk, 18–23. Logan: Utah State University Press.

Yancey, Kathleen Blake. 2015. "Introduction: Coming to Terms: Composition/Rhetoric, Threshold Concepts, and a Disciplinary Core." 2015. In *Naming What We Know: Threshold Concepts of Writing Studies,* edited by Linda Adler-Kassner and Elizabeth Wardle, xvii–xxxi. Logan: Utah State University Press.

Zawacki, Terry Myers. 2008. "Writing Fellows as WAC Change Agents: Changing What? Changing Whom? Changing How?" Special issue on writing fellows, *Across the Disciplines* 5. http://wac.colostate.edu/atd/fellows/zawacki.cfm.

Zipin, Lew. 2009. "Dark Funds of Knowledge, Deep Funds of Pedagogy: Exploring Boundaries between Lifewords and Schools." *Discourse: Studies in the Cultural Politics of Education* 30 (3): 317–31.

INDEX